Satan and His Daughter,
The Angel Liberty

Victor Hugo sur le rocher des proscrits
(Victor Hugo on the Rock of the Exiled), Jersey, summer of 1853,
photograph by Charles Hugo, Maison de Victor Hugo, Paris

VICTOR HUGO

Satan and His Daughter, The Angel Liberty

SELECTED VERSES FROM LA FIN DE SATAN

ILLUSTRATIONS BY ODILON REDON

TRANSLATION BY R.G. SKINNER

SWAN
ISLE
PRESS

CHICAGO, 2019

VICTOR HUGO (1802–85) was a great French poet, novelist, playwright, artist, and statesman. Living in exile on the islands of Jersey and Guernsey for eighteen years, the author of Les Misérables and The Hunchback of Notre Dame wrote some of his most influential work during that time. Highly esteemed for his poetry, La Fin de Satan was a work in progress at the time of his death and published posthumously.

RICHARD G. SKINNER is an independent scholar and poet.

Swan Isle Press, Chicago 60628
© 2019 by Swan Isle Press
Translation © R. G. Skinner
All rights reserved. Published 2019.
Printed in the United States of America
First Edition
23 22 21 20 19   1 2 3 4 5
ISBN-13: 978-0-9972287-3-1 (paperback)

Originally published as part of La Fin de Satan.
Translation is based on OEuvres complète de Victor Hugo, Poésie XI, La Fin de Satan. Dieu. Paris: Imprimerie nationale, 1911.

Library of Congress Cataloging-in-Publication Data
Names: Hugo, Victor, 1802-1885, author. | Redon, Odilon, 1840-1916, illustrator. | Skinner, R. G. (Richard G.) | Hugo, Victor, 1802-1885. Fin de Satan. | Hugo, Victor, 1802-1885. Dieu.
Title: Satan and His Daughter, The Angel Liberty : selected verses from La Fin de Satan / Victor Hugo ; illustrations by Odilon Redon ; translation by R.G. Skinner.
Description: First edition. | Chicago : Swan Isle Press, 2019. | "Translation is based on OEuvres complète de Victor Hugo, Poésie XI, La Fin de Satan. Dieu. Paris: Imprimerie nationale, 1911."
Identifiers: LCCN 2018038452 | ISBN 9780997228731 (paperback)
Subjects: LCSH: Hugo, Victor, 1802-1885--Translations into English. | BISAC: RELIGION / Mysticism. | POETRY / General. | POLITICAL SCIENCE / General.
Classification: LCC PQ2283 .P64 2018 | DDC 841/.7--dc23
LC record available at https://lccn.loc.gov/2018038452

Swan Isle Press gratefully acknowledges that this book was made possible, in part, with the generous support of the following:
EUROPE BAY GIVING TRUST
FRANCIS J. HIGGINS

The paper used in this publication meets the minimum requirements of the American National Standard for Information Sciences—Permanence of Paper for Printed Library Materials. ANSI/NISO Z39.48-1992.

www.swanislepress.com

To my wife, Cat O'Reilly

Contents

LIST OF ILLUSTRATIONS   *ix*

ACKNOWLEDGMENTS   *xiii*

INTRODUCTION   *xv*

Notes   xxix

STELLA   *1*

BEYOND THE EARTH   5

Beyond the Earth I
And Then There Was Night   7

Beyond the Earth II
Satan's Feather   19

Beyond the Earth III

I Satan in the Night   23
I, II
In the Air ◆ *Song of the Birds*   26
III-XVI   37

II The Angel Liberty   61
I, II, VII, VIII

DENOUEMENT   83

BIBLIOGRAPHY   85

LIST OF ILLUSTRATIONS

Pandore (Pandora), by Redon, oil on canvas (1910/1912), Courtesy National Gallery of Art, Washington. *(cover)*

Victor Hugo sur le rocher des proscrits (Victor Hugo on the Rock of the Exiled), Jersey, summer of 1853, photograph by Charles Hugo, Maison de Victor Hugo, Paris *(frontispiece)*

Ecce Lex, pen and ink, by Victor Hugo, Jersey 1854, Maison de Victor Hugo

Pélerin du monde sublunaire (Pilgrim of the sublunary world), from *Songes* (Dreams) by Redon, lithograph (1891), Courtesy National Gallery of Art, Washington.

Les Sciapodes: La tête le plus bas possible, c'est le secret du bonheur! (The Skiapods: The head as low as possible, that is the secret of happiness!), from *À Gustave Flaubert: Six dessins pour la Tentation de St Antoine* by Redon, lithograph (1889), Courtesy National Gallery of Art, Washington.

Gloire et louange à toi, Satan, dans les hauteurs, du ciel où tu régnas, et dans les profondeurs, de l'Enfer, où vaincu, tu rêves en silence! (Glory and praise to you, Satan, in the heights of heaven, where you reigned, and in the depths of hell, where, vanquished, you dream in silence!) from *Les Fleurs du Mal* by Baudelaire, lithograph by Redon (1890), Courtesy National Gallery of Art, Washington.

Et là-bas l'idole astrale, l'Apothéose (And yonder, the astral idol, the Apotheosis), from *Songes* (Dreams) by Redon, lithograph (1891), Courtesy National Gallery of Art, Washington.

St George et le Dragon (Saint George and the Dragon), by Redon, charcoal and pastel (1800s and c. 1891), Courtesy National Gallery of Art, Washington.

Le Liseur (The Reader), by Redon, lithograph (1892), Courtesy National Gallery of Art, Washington.

Tête d'Enfant avec Fleurs (Head of a Child with Flowers), by Redon, lithograph (1897), Courtesy National Gallery of Art, Washington.

Le Sphynx...mon regard que rien ne peut dévier, demeure tendu à travers les choses sur un horizon inaccessible. La Chimère: Moi, Je suis légère et joyeuse (The Sphinx: My gaze, which nothing can deflect passing through objects, remains fixed on an inaccessible horizon. The Chimera: As for me, I am light and joyful), from *À Gustave Flaubert: Six dessins pour la Tentation de St Antoine* by Redon, lithograph (1889), Courtesy National Gallery of Art, Washington.

L'Évocation de Roussel (Evocation of Roussel), by Redon, oil on canvas (c. 1912), Courtesy National Gallery of Art, Washington.

Passage d'une Âme (Passage of a Spirit), Frontispiece for *La Passante* (The Passer-by) by Adrien Remacle, etching by Redon, (1891), Courtesy National Gallery of Art, Washington.

Et le lia pour mille ans (And bound him a thousand years), from *L'Apocalypse de St Jean*, by Redon, lithograph (1899), Courtesy National Gallery of Art, Washington.

Et l'homme parut, interrogeant le sol d'où il sort et qui l'attire, il se fraya la voie vers de sombres clartés (And Man appeared; questioning the earth from which he emerged and which attracts him, he made his way toward somber brightness) from *Les Origines* (The Origins) by Redon, lithograph (1883), Courtesy National Gallery of Art, Washington.

Si par une nuit lourde et sombre, un bon chrétien, par charité, derrière quelque vieux décembre, enterré votre corps vanté (If on a close, dark night a good Christian, out of charity, behind some old ruin, buries your vaunted corpse) from *Les Fleurs du Mal* by Baudelaire, lithograph by Redon (1890), Courtesy National Gallery of Art, Washington.

Et celui qui était monté dessus se nommait la Mort (And he that sat upon him was named Death), from *L'Apocalypse de St Jean*, by Redon, lithograph (1899), Courtesy National Gallery of Art, Washington.

Il y eut peut-être une vision première essayée dans la fleur (There was perhaps a primal vision attempted in the flower) from *Les Origines* (The Origins) by Redon, lithograph (1883), Courtesy National Gallery of Art, Washington.

The Book of Light, by Redon, charcoal on tan paper (1893), Courtesy National Gallery of Art, Washington.

C'est le Diable (It is the Devil) from *La Tentation de St Antoine* by Flaubert, lithograph by Redon (1888), Courtesy National Gallery of Art, Washington.

Une femme revêtue du Soleil (A woman clothed with the sun) from *L'Apocalypse de St Jean*, by Redon, lithograph (1899), Courtesy National Gallery of Art, Washington.

Sous l'aile d'ombre, l'être noir appliquait une active morsure (Beneath the wing of shadow the black creature was biting fiercely) from *Songes* (Dreams) by Redon, lithograph (1891), Courtesy National Gallery of Art, Washington.

Puis l'ange prit l'encensoir (Then the angel took the censer) from *L'Apocalypse de St Jean*, by Redon, lithograph (1899), Courtesy National Gallery of Art, Washington.

La Sulamite (The Shulamite), by Redon, lithograph (1897), Courtesy National Gallery of Art, Washington.

La Mort: Mon ironie dépasse toutes les autres! (Death: My irony surpasses all others!) from *À Gustave Flaubert: Six dessins pour la Tentation de St Antoine* by Redon, lithograph (1889), Courtesy National Gallery of Art, Washington. .

Frontispiece (detail) for *À Gustave Flaubert: Six dessins pour la Tentation de St Antoine* by Redon, lithograph (1889), Courtesy National Gallery of Art, Washington.

Et il tombe du ciel une grande étoile ardente comme un flambeau (And there fell a great star from heaven burning as it were a lamp) from *L'Apocalypse de St Jean*, by Redon, lithograph (1899), Courtesy National Gallery of Art, Washington.

Et il avait dans sa main droit sept étoiles, et de sa bouch sortait une épée aiguë à deux tranchants (And he had in his right hand seven stars; and out of his mouth went a sharp two-edged sword) from *L'Apocalypse de St Jean*, by Redon, lithograph (1899), Courtesy National Gallery of Art, Washington.

La Hantise (The Obsession), by Redon, lithograph (1893), Courtesy National Gallery of Art, Washington.

Saint Sebastian, by Redon, oil on canvas (1910/1912), Courtesy National Gallery of Art, Washington.

Acknowledgments

I wish to express much appreciation to Matthew Loving and Blake Landor, past librarians at the University of Florida, for their help and encouragement throughout this project, to my publisher, David Rade, for his kindness and willingness to bring Victor Hugo's lesser-known masterworks to the reading public, and to the Maison de Victor Hugo, Paris, home to Charles Hugo's photograph, *Victor Hugo sur le rocher des proscrits*, and Victor Hugo's pen and ink, *Ecce Lex*. I would also like to acknowledge that the Odilon Redon illustrations appearing in this book are courtesy of the National Gallery of Art, Washington, and its NGA Images program.

Introduction

Satan, and His Daughter, The Angel Liberty consists of verses excerpted from Victor Hugo's book-length, visionary poem *La Fin de Satan* (The End of Satan). A work both religious and political, it was written on the islands of Jersey and Guernsey, Hugo's homes during his political exile (1852–1870) at the hands of France's Emperor Napoleon III. This long poem, never quite finished, was meant, in part, as an indictment of the "three scourges of the Old World"–war, capital punishment, and prison–and begins and ends with the poignant story of Satan and his daughter, Liberty. Created by God from a feather left behind following Satan's banishment, the angel is the embodiment of compassion and forgiveness as she attempts to convince her father to give up his evil ways and return to Heaven. For his part, Satan reveals, through a despairing soliloquy, his bitterness and intent on revenge, and yet his love for God, and a desire for forgiveness and redemption. These verses typified the prevailing French Romantic tradition of creating religious myths more in tune with ideas of the times.[1] Hugo wished to repudiate the Catholic doctrine of the Immaculate Conception,[2] believing, instead, that all people are born free of original sin, and that those in Hell are not doomed for all eternity, but can be forgiven and redeemed.

The angel Liberty represented, as well, Hugo's years of fighting imperialism, having become the voice of France and the cause of freedom everywhere. His writing was meant to teach, whether through his anti-imperial diatribes, his poetry, or his novels such as *Les Misérables*, also written during these exile years. At the time, in a letter written from Guernsey on June 7th, 1856 to Barthélemy (Prosper) Enfantin, social-reformer and co-founder of Saint-Simonianism, he referred to *La Fin de Satan* and its companion epic, *Dieu* (God):

> The ideal is the real. Like you, I live with my eyes fixed on
> a vision. To do my best so far as my strength will allow to
> help mankind, that hapless crowd of brothers we have
> there who are walking in darkness, and I endeavor, bound
> to the chain myself, to aid my fellow-travelers, by my
> example as a man in the present, and by my writings as a
> poet in the future....I shall go beyond the things of this
> world...to carry the crowd to certain altitudes; yet I'm
> well aware that there is little air there which it can breathe.
> I therefore wish it to rest awhile before I make it attempt
> a fresh ascent.[3]

When these two poems were in their early stages, he had told another friend, his protégé Auguste Vacquerie, that this work was not meant for momentary success. Although Hugo saw his role in this world as champion for liberty against tyranny, his long exile in the English channel was carrying him "beyond the things of this world," and just as the message of *Dieu* was that organized religion perpetuated crimes against humanity, that God consists of Light and Love but is unreachable, the essence of *La Fin de Satan* is that of compassion, that all can be forgiven, even Evil.

Three years after *La Fin de Satan* was published, his friend and correspondent, the English poet A.C. Swinburne, wrote of it and the story of Satan and his daughter:

> More than thirty years have elapsed between the announcement and the appearance of the great religious poem which has done for the nineteenth century what was done for the thirteenth by the *Divina Commedia* and for the seventeenth by *Paradise Lost*....[All] demur, all question, all doubt is swallowed up in wonder and delight at the glory and the beauty of the indefatigable song. The flight of the fallen archangel towards the dying sun through chaos is given with that all but unique effect which Dante alone could hitherto achieve by alternation or combination of the very homeliest with the very sublimest images or comparisons....
>
> ...I pass over the exquisite verses which embody the strange and subtle myth of the birth of the angel Liberty from the glance of God upon the remaining feather of the fallen archangel's fallen wings which had not shared his fall into the abyss of hell....
>
> The prelude of the third book is one of the sublimest poems which compose the mythic or symbolic part of the poet's work. In all the vast compass of that world of song where only we can find its like we can find nothing more majestic in its ardour of imagination than the myth of the angel Liberty, the description of her descent, the pictures of winter's everlasting and eternal night, of the spectre which resists and perishes, of the supreme appeal which evokes, at last, a word from the sleeping spirit of evil. Every line, every word, is laden with significant loveliness and alive with vivid emotion.[4]

This book extracts what I consider the gem of the epic work originally entitled *Satan Pardonné* (Satan Forgiven). Given that the name "Satan" was retained in the final title, and that the poem begins and ends with this story, I believe that it was Hugo's primary focus. The idea of liberty, of freedom, was utmost in Hugo's mind throughout his exile, and especially in the early years when he began this poem. It seems fitting that these particular verses be given prominence, featuring as they do an angel of that name. At the time, Hugo was still dealing with the loss of his daughter, Léopoldine, his favorite child, whose death a decade earlier still haunted him. He had dedicated to her the verses, "À celle qui est restée en France" (To She Who Remained In France), the epilogue to a two-volume collection of poems, *Les Contemplations*, written contemporaneously with *La Fin de Satan* and *Dieu*. This work also contained a poem addressed directly to her, "Demain dès l'aube" (Tomorrow, at Dawn). Hugo only learned of her death from a newspaper story while traveling with his mistress. Perhaps the angel represented his daughter from whom he sought forgiveness for being somehow complicit in her death. He was given some respite when he was able to conjure her up once at the start of his séance sessions the second year on Jersey, eliciting from her the assurance that she was in a good place. Rather than this story being buried in four parts, as in the original work, it has been brought together here, in a single narrative that might not have been as accessible or apparent to those who were working their way through my original published translation of selections from this work, *God and The End of Satan/Dieu et La Fin de Satan*.

Much of Victor Hugo's poetry is comprised of Alexandrines, pairs of rhymed, twelve-syllable verses, each line containing two six-syllable phrases or clauses, called *hemistiches*, separated by a break called a *cæsura*. Each couplet had either masculine or feminine endings, and alternated from one to the other throughout the course of the poem. The rules for this form are very strict, and were refined to perfection by the time of the dramatist Racine (1639-1699). Most probably it is derived from a collection of romances, collected in the twelfth century, based on the exploits of Alexander the Great. There is also a theory that the form was invented by the twelfth-century poet Alexander of Paris. Normally, each line of an Alexandrine ends with a punctuation mark ending a sentence or phrase, creating a natural pause called an end-stop. When a sentence or phrase continued onto the next line without a pause, it was called *enjambment*, and in the classical Alexandrine was considered a serious transgression. However, near the end of the eighteenth century André Chénier made extensive use of *enjambment*, greatly influencing the following generations of romantic poets who discovered his work when first published in 1819, and who saw in its use a greater freedom of expression. When a young Victor Hugo discovered it, he was already considering the use of other poetic forms, under the influence of his friend Sainte-Beuve, and believed it conveyed a greater sense of prose, an effect he wished to create. As a result, his already narrative poetry became not only conversational, but read like novels. He exploited *enjambment* to the full in his 1830 drama *Hernani*, whose opening lines read:

> *Doña J.* [*Seule.*] Serait-ce déjà lui? C'est bien l'escalier
> Derobé. Vite, ouvrons.

> [Entre Don Carlos]　　　　　　　　Bonjour, beau cavalier.

> (Is he already here? It must be by the secret
> staircase. Quick, let us open up.

> Greetings, handsome cavalier.)[5]

The immediate *enjambment*, where "Derobé" carries the phrase past the line break, had the force of a manifesto and precipitated riots because of its divergence from classical form. In his 1827 revolutionary preface to the unproduced drama *Oliver Cromwell*, which became a veritable manifesto for the Romantic movement, Hugo had anticipated this violation of form on a large scale when he characterized the Alexandrine as monotonous:

> Had we the right to say what, in our opinion, should
> be the style of dramatic poetry, we would declare our
> liking for...verse that makes bold at fitting times to change
> the place of the *cæsura* and thereby avoid monotony of
> Alexandrines; verse that prefers the *enjambement*, which
> lengthens out the line, than to the inversion of phrases that
> confuses the sense....[6];

Where, in *Dieu* and *La Fin de Satan*, Hugo had broken the rules of the Alexandrine, his literary executors had often seen fit to correct them by adding verses or changing the gender of rhymes. But in the end, the continued use of *enjambment*, and Hugo's shift from the two-*hemistich* structure to a three-part line called *alexandrin ternaire* led ultimately to the *vers libre* and prose poetry of Arthur Rimbaud. Rimbaud in his turn called *Les Misérables* an immense poem in prose, and one can find in Hugo's next masterpiece, the novel *Les Travailleurs de la Mer* (The Toilers of the Sea), where Hugo is freed altogether from the constrictions of the rhymed couplet, a litany of winds that rivals his description of the Pyrenean cirque, Gavarnie, in *Dieu*, or the Great Flood, in *La Fin de Satan*:

> ...the wind of the Bay of Bengal, which flows as far north as
> Nijni-Novogorod, penetrating the triangle of sheds in which

the fair of Asia is held; the wind of the Cordilleras, agita-
tor of the great waves and the huge forests; the wind of the
Australian Archipeligo, where the hunters for honey dislodge
the hives of wild bees which are hidden under the axillæ of
the branches of the giant eucalyptus; the sirocco, the mistral,
the hurricane, the dry winds, the penetrating winds, the flood
winds, the torrid winds, those which scatter the dust of the
plains of Brazil upon the streets of Genoa; those which obey
the diurnal rotation, and those which blow in opposition to it,
and which caused Herrera to say: "*Malo viento torna contra el
sol*" (Evil comes from turning away from the sun)...[7]

or earlier in his tale, this description of night at sea:

An indescribable roof of darkness; a deep obscurity which
no diver can penetrate; light mingled with that obscurity, an
indescribable, subdued, and sombre light; pulverized light; is
it a seed? is it ashes? millions of torches, but no light; a vast
ignition which keeps its own secret, a diffusion of fire in dust
which has the appearance of flying sparks stopped in their
course; the disorder of the whirlwind with the immobility of
the sepulchre, the problem presenting a precipitous opening,
the enigma alternately showing and concealing its face, the
infinite masked with darkness; such is night.[8]

Ironically, one of Hugo's original literary executors, writer
Paul Meurice, would have concurred. When he was preparing a
new edition of Hugo's complete works for the Imprimerie natio-
nale, twenty years after Hugo's death, in 1905, he conveyed to his
assistant and protégé, Gustave Simon, the joy he felt at making
new discoveries in the manuscripts: "Ah! my friend! when I think
there are still magnificent pages, bits of philosophy, fragments of

poetry, *Choses vues*, wonderful descriptions that I reserve for the *Travailleurs de la Mer...*"[9]

I have tried to keep to the spirit of Hugo's desire for his poetry to read like poetic prose. Earlier works whose translators have also eschewed a rhymed translation (for fear of losing the meaning), or rendered Alexandrines or other poetic forms in prose, include de Nerval's translation of Goethe's *Faust*, Chateaubriand's of Milton's *Paradise Lost*, François-Victor Hugo's of the works of Shakespeare, and more recently Richard Howard's of Baudelaire's *Les Fleurs du Mal*.

Two points of clarification will perhaps be helpful to the reader of this fable. When A.C. Swinburne speaks of "the spectre which resists and perishes," he is referring not to Satan, but to Liberty's adversary, Isis-Lilith, a demonic presence who facilitates Satan's evil deeds throughout the original poem. It is she who ultimately perishes at the hands of the angel Liberty, a necessary step in Liberty's quest to save her father. I exclude Isis-Lilith from this work, choosing to portray strictly the relationship between Satan and his daughter. This will explain the missing stanzas, III through VI, in the section entitled "The Angel Liberty." In excluding certain of these passages, we fail initially to reconcile, on the one hand, Satan's early inability to sleep, and his later sleeping state when encountering his daughter. At this later time, as Liberty explains, "...so that I may speak to you, [God] lets you sleep. Because, Father, for your eyes, alas! the firmament can half-open only in dream!"

The second point of clarification concerns the ending. The "Denouèment" is found on folio (page) 279r of the MS, written on the back of a large envelope. The word "Denouèment" is written over the word "Fin" (End), indicating that Hugo wished to finish the poem with these verses. Because Hugo never completed the poem, he never resolved a slight contradiction in the text. After Liberty has finished pleading her case to her father in "The Angel Liberty," he appears to accept forgiveness. Yet at the end, in the "Denouèment," Satan still expresses his tormented belief that God hates him and thus has not pardoned him. At that point God does forgive him. Perhaps it's simply a matter of Satan requiring a direct communication from God, rather than through his emissary, their daughter the angel Liberty. We don't know what Hugo's final solution would have been.

As a final detail of interest, the poem "Song of the Birds," which I retain as verse, was placed by Hugo in the midst of Satan's soliloquy in order to give the reader a brief respite from the unrelenting pathos. As indicated on the first MS page of this poem, folio 203r, it was started April 15th, 1860, on Guernsey, atop the turreted Victoria Tower with its spectacular view of the island, a place Hugo often visited, and was written over a five-day period.

The illustrations of Odilon Redon, created a generation later, have been chosen to accompany these verses due to their striking affinity to the tale, and the artist's own feelings of alienation and exile. Although no direct evidence of influence links Odilon Redon to Hugo, the Paris-based artist was particularly drawn to literature, and had to be aware of the latter's writings, as well as his extraordinary artwork. Hugo, Redon's senior by thirty-eight years, dominated all of French literature until his death at age eighty-three. At that time Redon's close friend, Mallarmé, noted the crisis in French verse at Hugo's passing. Redon did share the poet's dark vision, particularly in his *noirs* (the dark work of his earlier years),[10] and in his own writing. Despite the fact that many of the illustrations in this volume were meant for the work of Baudelaire, Flaubert, and

St. John the Devine, they match well Hugo's verses which were very much in keeping with the tone of *Les Fleurs du mal* (The Flowers of Evil), *La Tentation de Saint Antoine* (The Temptation of Saint Anthony), and The Book of Revelation. Hugo even spoke of the poem *Dieu* as his "Apocalypse." Both poems were a product of those séances held at his home on Jersey, his ruminations on the cosmos as he sat overlooking the sea, and the more temporal concern with freedom.

Although there was an absence of Hugo's books in Redon's library at his death, there were noteworthy parallels between the two men in their lives and preoccupations. Each of them had lost his first-born son. Both shared that interest in the occult and the esoteric, perhaps as a way of helping them grieve their losses. Hugo's writing and Redon's painting were at times likened to William Blake's late visionary writing and art, and in their graphic imagery both were influenced by Rembrandt, Piranesi, Goya, and Dürer. Just as Hugo in exile used free-association in his spiritist writing and his artwork, Redon later in life would place charcoal or pigment randomly on paper and create according to the shapes suggested accidentally. He was particularly drawn to Delacroix, who had been part of Hugo's circle in his youth, and had called Hugo the "prince of poets." Like Hugo, Delacroix, and other romantics, Redon was captivated by medieval architecture (Hugo's *Notre-Dame de Paris* was in part a plea for a restoration of the famous cathedral), but it was particularly Delacroix who represented the Romantic world of the imagination, of a longing for a distant past. In many of Redon's *noirs*, "…the theme of solitude predominates, revealing his continuing affiliation with the Romantics, both in subject and in barren settings that emphasize human insignificance."[11] Later in life he would call his *noirs* his *ombres* (ghosts) because of their highly personal nature and other-worldly subjects.

Perhaps most striking is Redon's own sense of exile experienced in his youth, banished to the family estate due to his epilepsy: "I dearly wish that...I had been born amid the waves I have often contemplated since from the cliff tops of Brittany, in suffering and sorrow; a place without a homeland, over an abyss...."[12] As Redon, the exiled teenager, looked across the water from Brittany in the late 1850's, Hugo, the exiled poet, from his studio atop his new home on the island of Guernsey, still working on *Dieu* and *La Fin de Satan*, looked back across the water toward that same northern coast of France.

In literature, Redon did find melancholy protagonists with whom to identify, in Lamartine's *Raphael*, Chateaubriand's *René*, and Senancour's *Obermann*, works that matched his early feeling of solitude, isolation, and exile, and offered a sense of sublime transcendence, as did Rousseau's *La nouvelle Héloïse*. Maurice de Guérin's *Le Centaure* was a work that remained essential to Redon throughout his life, and it was in the former's *Journal*, purchased in 1868, that Redon first discovered a kindred soul who also felt out of step with his times. Here he would have read de Guérin write of Hugo:

> It is needless to say that all that comes from Hugo is remarkable, and bears the stamp of power. There is something in the temper of his genius so surprising, so brilliant, so bewildering, that after reading one of his works, whether it be drama, ode, or romance, we are filled with wonder, our souls are deeply moved, and our minds greatly excited. All these compositions stir some of the inmost fibers of humanity or probe some hidden depth.[13]

However, had Redon found Hugo congenial during his formative years, he would nevertheless have parted ways with the poet and his later sympathy with certain aspects of Saint-Simonianism, which emphasized science, positivism, and progress in general. Yet, if in fact Redon, who had produced a work entitled "Descent into Hell" in 1873, had read the story of Satan in Hugo's *La Fin de Satan*, published in 1886, when Redon was forty-six and still in the throes of the alienation that produced his *noirs*, he might well have felt a kinship with the melancholy protagonist.

There are other ways in which Hugo could have touched Redon as he did the lives of those around the young artist. Poet Octave Giraud, born on the island of Guadeloupe, though nostalgic for colonial times, advocated the abolition of slavery, which brought him the attention and support of Hugo, for many years an advocate of the same cause. In 1854, Hugo drew several versions of the image opposite, capturing the inhumanity of capitol punishment (another of the themes of *La Fin de Satan*), and in 1859 allowed its use to protest the hanging in America of the abolitionist, John Brown: "Anything that furthers the great aim, Liberty, is a duty as far as I am concerned, and I shall be happy if this drawing...helps keep ever-present in people's souls the memory of this liberator of our black brethren...."[14] Redon was in close contact with Giraud and his liberal circle in Bordeaux, where he was then based prior to his move to Paris, and although his early writings and artwork were more emotional than intellectual, they represented the idealistic and democratic views of Hugo, and of Giraud and his opposition to the materialism of the Second Empire. Devoted to new literature, Giraud's group was particularly interested in works like Hugo's *Les Misérables* that addressed social issues.

Ecce Lex, pen and ink, by Victor Hugo, Jersey 1854,
Maison de Victor Hugo

Later opposed to naturalism and the aesthetic expression
of scientific materialism with its new interest in enhancing the
spiritual, Redon became an advocate of Symbolism, the literary
and artistic movement of suggestion and mystery which linked

Romanticism to Surrealism. He was one of the most admired, sought-after illustrators of Symbolist works by Baudelaire, Mallarmé, and others, even creating images for Mallarmé's seminal "Un coup de dés" which came to light years after their completion.[15] Fellow Symbolist artist Maurice Denis called Redon "our Mallarmé," due to his close friendship with the poet and the intrinsic quality of his own writing. The long titles to his artwork, found for example in his collections *Songes* and *Les Origines*, some of which are featured in this book, were Symbolist in nature, and much admired by Mallarmé.[16]

It is through the lens of Symbolism that today we view the imagery and words of Redon, dubbed "the prince of dreams" by his fellow Symbolists, as was Hugo called the "prince of poets" by his Romantic contemporaries. Yet Hugo viewed himself a dreamer, as well. In the manuscript of *La Fin de Satan*, near the end of the first section of verse describing Satan's fall, "Et Nox Facta Est" (And Then There Was Night), which begins this volume, Hugo wrote and then scratched out "Words of he who dreams while writing this book" (Paroles de celui qui songe en écrivant ce livre).[17] Later, he wrote from Guernsey to Franz Stevens, a young Belgian poet: "I dwell in this immense dream of the ocean. I am gradually becoming a somnambulist of the sea; and in face of all these stupendous phenomena and all this vast living thought in which I lose myself, I end up by being a sort of witness of God."[18] Scholars such as Jean Gaulmier and Florian Rodari see in Hugo's poetic œuvre the seeds of the symbolist work of Baudelaire, Rimbaud, and Mallarmé, and specifically in *Dieu* and *La Fin de Satan*, verses that anticipate the modern poetry of Surrealism and beyond.

These passages of verse that make up *Satan and His Daughter, The Angel Liberty*, now in prose form, are at the core of the moving narrative found dispersed throughout the original work and the previous translated edition of selections. In this slimmer volume, that Hugo fable is now presented in a unique narrative literary format, and to help set the tone, the mood, of that narrative is that other creative leap, to Redon's illustrations, a sort of posthumous collaboration between Hugo and Redon that yields its own insights and, can we say, surprises.

Notes

1. John Andrew Frey, *A Victor Hugo Encyclopedia* (Westport, Connecticut: Greenwood Press, 1999), 99.

2. E.H. and A.M. Blackmore, from an unpublished MS of *Dieu* translation.

3. Victor Hugo, *The Letters of Victor Hugo: From Exile, and After the Fall of the Empire*, edited by Paul Meurice (Boston: Houghton, Mifflin & Co., 1898), 140.

4. Algernon Charles Swinburne, *Studies in prose and poetry* (London: Chatto & Windus, 1894), 170-71, 173, 180.

5. Victor Hugo, *Dramas / Victor Hugo*; volume I, *Hernani*, translated by I.G. Burnham (Philadelphia: George Barrie, 1896), 19.

6. Victor Hugo, *Dramas / Victor Hugo*; volume IX, *Oliver Cromwell*, translated by I.G. Burnham (Philadelphia: George Barrie, 1896), 84.

7. Victor Hugo, *Novels / Victor Hugo*; volume III, *The Toilers of the Sea*, translated by Mary W. Artois (Philadelphia: George Barrie, 1892), 182.

8. Ibid., 122-23

9. Gustave Simon, "Paul Meurice—Souvenirs Intimes," *La Revue de Paris*. Treizième Année. Tome Troisième. Mai–Juin. (Paris: Bureaux de la Revue de Paris, 1906), 90.

> —Ah! mon ami! quand je pense qu'il y a encore de magnifiques pages, des morceaux de philosophie, des fragments de poésie, des *Choses vues*, des descriptions admirables que je réserve pour les *Travailleurs de la Mer*...

10. In Redon's later years, when he was married and receiving some acclaim from the critics, he began working in color. After this point in his career there was rarely a return to a dark palette.

11. Douglas W. Druick et al., *Odilon Redon: prince of dreams, 1840-1916* (Chicago: Art Institute of Chicago; Amsterdam: Van Gogh Museum; London: Royal Academy of Arts; New York: H.N. Abrams, Inc., 1994), 61.

12. Dario Gamboni, *The Brush and the Pen: Odilon Redon and Literature* (Chicago: University of Chicago Press, 2011), 12.

13. Maurice de Guérin, *Journal of Maurice de Guérin*, translated by Jessie P. Frothingham (New York: Dodd, Mead, and Company, 1901), 82-83.

14. Florian Rodari, *Shadows of a Hand: the drawings of Victor Hugo*, translated by Judith Hayward and Mark Hutchinson (London: The Drawing Center New York in association with Merrell Holberton Publishers, 1998), 122.

15. Lloyd James Austin, *Poetic Principles and Practices: occasional papers on Baudelaire, Mallarmé, and Valéry*, chapter 8, "Mallarmé and the visual arts" (1972) (Cambridge, New York: Cambridge University Press, 1987), 135.

16. Hilton Kramer, "Art View: Symbolism—in search of a style." New York Times (Arts), January 4, 1981.

17. Victor Hugo, *Œuvres Complètes de Victor Hugo, Poésie XI, La Fin de Satan. Dieu.* (Paris: Imprimerie nationale, 1911), 274.

18. Victor Hugo, *The Letters*, 137-138.

Stella

"...this divine smile lit up the heavens."

Stella

I had fallen asleep that night near the seashore, when a fresh breeze awakened me from my dreams. I opened my eyes, and spied at the horizon the morning star—infinite, lovely, and aglow with beams of soft, pure light. Aquilon fled, bearing the tempest, whilst the glowing orb turned the clouds to down. She gleamed, resonant with thought, with life. She calmed the reef where the wave breaks; and I believed I was seeing a soul through a pearl. It was still night, yet the darkness reigned in vain, as this divine smile lit up the heavens.

The light cast a silver shimmer upon the top of the listing mast whose ship was black, but whose sail glowed white. Seagulls, perched upon a cliff, gazed solemnly upon the star as upon a celestial bird formed from a spark. The ocean, resembling a vast multitude, approached her, and, roaring in a whisper, seemingly afraid of making her flee, watched her gleam. An ineffable love filled the land. The green grass at my feet trembled, bewildered; birds spoke to one another in their nests; a waking flower told me: this star is my sister. And whilst dawn raised its long, pleated veil, I heard a voice, which came from the star, say:—I am the star that arrives first. I am the one thought to dwell within the tomb, but who has since left. I have shone upon Sinai, I have shone upon Mount Taygetos; I am the fiery stone of gold which God casts, as with a sling, upon the black brow of night. I am what is reborn when a world is destroyed.

O nations! I am ardent poetry. I have blazed over Moses and I have flared over Dante. The lion, Ocean, loves me. I am coming. Arise, virtue, courage, faith! Thinkers, spirits, sentinels, mount the tower! Eyelids, open, light up, eyes, Earth, move your furrows, life, awaken sonority. Up, you who sleep!—for the one who follows me, the one who sends me forth, is the angel Liberty, the immense Light!

Victor Hugo—Jersey, 31 August, 1853
(from *Les Châtiments*, Book Six)

Beyond the Earth

❧

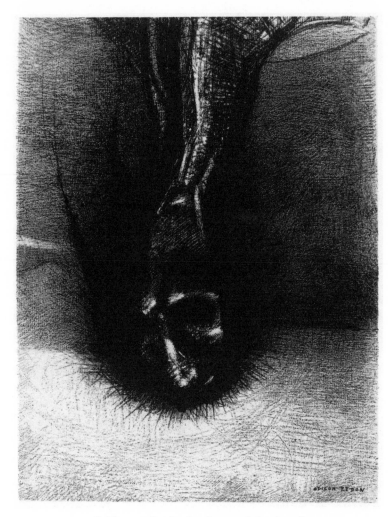

"...like a wedge, his head opened the abyss."

Beyond the Earth I

AND THEN THERE WAS NIGHT

I

FOR FOUR THOUSAND YEARS HE WAS FALLING INTO THE abyss. He had not yet been able to seize an outcropping, nor once raise his massive brow. He plunged into the darkness and mist, frightened, alone; and behind him, in the eternal nights, fell more slowly the feathers of his wings. He plummeted, thunderstruck, full of gloom, silent, and mournful, his mouth open and his feet pointed toward the Heavens, the horror of the gulf imprinted on his livid face. He cried:—Death!—his fists outstretched toward the empty darkness. This word later became 'Man' and was named 'Cain.'

He was falling. Suddenly a rock struck his hand; he held to it, as a dead man embraces his tomb, and stopped. Someone, from on high, cried out to him:—Fall! The suns will die out around you, accursed one.— and the voice was lost in the immense horror. And, turning pale, he looked toward the eternal dawn. The suns were distant, but shone still. Satan lifted his head and said, raising his arms:—Liar!—This word later became the soul of Judas. Like bronze gods upright upon their pilasters, he waited a thousand years, his eyes fixed upon the stars.

The suns were distant, but were shining as ever. A thunderbolt then roared in the cold and voiceless heavens. Satan laughed, and spat at the thunder. The cosmos, filled by the visionary darkness, shuddered. This spittle later became Barabbas. Then, a passing wind made him fall further.

II

The fall of the damned one began once again—terrifying, overcast, and pierced with luminous holes like a sieve, the sky full of suns vanished, the light trembled, and into the night this giant plummeted headlong, naked, sinister, and dragged down by the weight of his crime; and like a wedge, his head opened the abyss. Lower! Lower! Ever lower! All, at his approach, fled him; no obstacle could he seize in passing, neither a mountain, nor a crumbling rock, nor a stone—nothing but gloom. Terrified, he closed his eyes. When he reopened them, only three suns shone, and the darkness had eroded the firmament. All the other suns were dead.

III

A rock immerged from the black fog, like an arm drawing near. He took hold, and alighted on the mountain peaks. Then the dreadful Being, who is called Never, began to think, lowering his brow to his criminal hands. Like three eyes, the three suns watched him from afar; but he did not return their gaze. Space resembled the plains on earth in the evening, when the horizon that sinks and recedes darkens beneath the white eyes of the spectral twilight. Long beams crawled to the feet of this great exile. Behind him, his shadow filled the infinite. The summits of chaos merged.

"Suddenly he found himself sprouting horrible wings;..."

Suddenly he found himself sprouting horrible wings; he saw himself becoming a monster, the angel in him dying, as the rebel in him felt growing trepidation. He let his shoulder, once luminous, tremble with the hideous cold of the membranous wing, and, crossing his arms, raising his head, this outlaw, as if growing taller in the face of this insult, alone in these depths congested by his ruin, looked fixedly at the cavern of night. The blackness began to slowly spread in this nothingness. The opaque shadow closed the gaping sky; and, beyond the last headland, the three suns merged their radiances, making a threefold fissure in this dark window. It appeared to be the three wheels of a chariot of fire shattered after some battle in the high firmaments. And the mountains emerged from the fog like the prows of ships.

Very well—shouted Satan—so be it! I can still see! He shall have the blue sky, and I, myself, the black. Does he believe I shall go weeping to his gate? I despise him. Three suns, that is enough. What does it matter to me! I hate the day, the azure, the sunlight, the perfume!

Suddenly he gave a start, for now there remained but one sun.

IV

The abyss was becoming obliterated. There were no more forms. The obscurity seemed to expand in an enormous wave, creating a vague feeling of being submerged. It became that which is no longer, that which disappears, becomes hidden; and one could not have said, in this deep horror, whether this was the frightening vestige of a mystery or of a world, like a hazy fog where the dream flees, or whether it called itself Shipwreck or Night; and the archangel felt that he was becoming a phantom. He

10

said:—Hell!—This word later created Sodom. And the voice from above slowly repeated:—Accursed one! Around you the suns shall die out.

And already the sun was nothing but a star.

V

And everything was slowly disappearing beneath a veil. The archangel became faint-hearted; Satan shuddered. He sprang towards the star that flickered, pale, on the horizon, leaping from one peak to another. Then, though he detested these bestial wings, which were for him the dress of prison, just as a bird flies from bush to bush, so this wretched convict took wing from mountain to mountain, and began to hasten towards this punition.

He ran, he flew, he cried out:—Golden star! Brother! Wait for me! I am coming! Do not die out yet! Do not leave me alone!— Thus did the monster clear the first lakes of this dead vastness, this ancient, empty chaos, already stagnating, and plunge into the dismal depths.

The star was now but a spark. He entered further into the all-embracing darkness, was thrust, thrown, hurled into the night, scaled the miry mountain whose moist crest glistened, and whose base swayed in the depths of cesspools, and, mournful, looked before him. The spark was no more than a red speck at the bottom of the dark gulf.

VI

Just as twilight overtakes the archer in his turret, stooped over the wall between two battlements, so does Satan lean over from the height of the mountain, and begin to savagely blow upon

"Just as twilight overtakes the archer in his turret,..."

the star, as on embers, hoping to make it gleam, his fierce nostrils flaring with the agonized effort. The breath which came from his lungs dwells on Earth today and is called 'Hurricane.' At this gust of wind, a great uproar disturbed the darkness, that ocean which no Being inhabits and which no fire illuminates; the nearby mountains fled, and monstrous, fearful Chaos rose up and began to howl:—Jehovah! Jehovah!—The infinite half-opened, rent like a fabric, but nothing stirred in the mournful star; and the accursed one, crying:—Do not go out! I am coming! I shall arrive!—resumed his desperate flight.

And the glaciers, mingling with the nights that resemble them, turned belly-up like cowed beasts, and the dark whirlwinds and the hideous chasms recoiled in terror, whilst above them, flying towards the star as an arrow towards its target, passed, rageful and gaunt, this terrible supplicant.

And ever since it saw this ghastly flight, this bitter, unfathomable gulf, frightened like a fleeing man, keeps forever an air of horror and madness, so dreadful was it to see fly, in the immense darkness, opening its hideous wings far from the heavens, this bat of the eternal dungeon!

VII

He flew for ten thousand years. For ten thousand years, straining his ghastly neck and his frenzied hands, he flew without finding a height on which to rest. At times the star appeared to die out and be eclipsed, and the horror of the tomb would make the angel shudder; then a pale, dark light would reappear, vague and obscure, and, joyous, he would say:—I must hurry!—Around him soared the birds of the north wind. With hardly a pause, the infinite one renewed his efforts afresh. His flight into this sea described an immense circle. The night watched flee his horrible talons; and as a cloud feels its eddies subside, he felt his strength desert him in the abyss. Winter murmured:—Tremble!—and the blackness said:—Suffer!—Finally he saw, in the distance, a lurid summit casting a great light into the darkness. Satan, like a swimmer making a supreme effort, stretched his bare, taloned wings, and, pale ghost, breathless, broken, spent, and steaming with sweat, fell to the edge of the rugged scarp.

VIII

The sun that was dying in the abyss was there. Without a wind to revive it, the star in the depths of the mist slowly cooled and faded, becoming dull. Its sinister roundness was visible in the night; and in this ghastly silence, one could see its ulcers of fire decreasing beneath a leprosy of shadows. The coal of an extinct world, a torch blown out by God, its fissures still showed a little fire as if, through holes in the skull, one could see the soul. In the center flickered and crawled a flame which at times licked the outer edges, and from each crater issued forth some rays of light which trembled like flaming swords, and then soundlessly vanished, as do dreams. The star was nearly black. The archangel was so weary that he had neither voice nor breath, alas!

But the star was perishing beneath his fierce gaze. It was dying. It fought. At times, from the lightless orifices in this cold gloom it launched scorching floods, reddened masses, smoking mountains, and rocks all frothing with primeval light, as if this giant of life and light, absorbed by the mist where everything vanishes, did not wish to die without insulting the night, without spitting its lava in the face of the gloom. Around it time and space, number and form, and sound expired, creating a formidable,

14

"...revealing in the distance a thousand funereal forms,..."

"...the Sage whose face is lit by a reflection from the abyss."

black nothingness. The barren void raised its head out of the pit. Suddenly, from the heart of the star, a fierce jet of sulfur, like the frantic outcry of the dying, shot out, startling, radiant, splendid, unexpected, enormous, revealing in the distance a thousand funereal forms, illuminating, in the far reaches of obscurity, the monstrous portals of the infinite deep. The spectacles, which night and vast space create, appeared. Satan, bewildered, breathless, his eye dazzled and full of this lightning, beat his wings, opened his hands, then trembled, and cried:—Despair! Everything is growing dim!—

And the archangel understood that, like a sinking ship's mast, he was drowning in a flood of darkness. He folded his wings with their talons of stone, wrung his hands, and the star died out.

IX

Now, near the heavens, at the edge of the pit where nothing changes, a pure, white feather, which had escaped from the wings of the archangel, sat fluttering, precariously. The angel before whom a dazzling dawn was breaking, saw it, gathered it up, and said, his gaze resting on the sublime sky:

—Lord, should this feather also go into the abyss?—God, absorbed in Being and in Life, turned, and said:—Do not cast down that which has not fallen.

Dark caves of the past, portals from a time without dates, without light, somber and immeasurable, eons prior to man, chaos, heavens, a world, terrible and full of mysterious Beings, O dreadful fog where the preadamites appeared, dwelling in the limitless gloom, who can sound you, chasms, times unknown! The thinker, the magus, who, like the poor, goes barefoot out of respect for the One we can not imagine, mines the depths and the origins and the epochs, explores and seeks beyond the Colossi, further than what the heavens now witness, turns pale as he reaches things long suspected, and, by uncovering the sunless years, and the layers of days, worlds and emptinesses, discovers monstrous dead ages beneath these immense centuries. And so it is that the Sage dreams in the depths of night, the Sage whose face is lit by a reflection from the abyss.

Beyond the Earth II

SATAN'S FEATHER

THE FEATHER, THE SOLE REMNANT OF THE WINGS OF THE archangel engulfed in eternal night, still lay on the brink of the dark abyss. The dead thus sometimes leave behind them something of themselves at the threshold of mournful night, some kind of vague and somber light, which persists. Had this feather a soul? Who knows? It had a strange appearance; it lay there and shone—it was made of fallen light. The angels furtively came to look, for it reminded them of the great Torchbearer; they marveled at it, thinking of that Being once so beautiful, now more hideous than the hydra and the rattlesnake. They thought of Satan whose fatal whiteness, first the delight, then the dread of the blue heavens, became monstrous to the point of making him the equal of God. This feather reawakened the breadth of that Angel, colossal and haughty.

It covered the rock with magnificent lightning-flashes; sometimes the Seraphim, too fearful to approach, recoiled before these shallows where the soul is transformed into a dragon, blinded by its enormous light. A flame seemed to float in the down of this feather; and one sensed, seeing it shiver, that it had once been part of a rebellious wing. Day and night, tender faith, atheist audacity, curiosity of the abysses, limitless flights, braving all hazards and fates—the wave and the air, majestic wisdom, madness—all palpitated faintly in this immense plume. But in its ineffable and voiceless quivering, with the breath of the abyss, with the wind of the firmament, one still felt more of love than of tempest.

Whilst He, who in His goodness ponders all, was now deep in thought upon the eternal summit, the feather of the greatest of the angels, rejected out of conscience and to preserve peace, trembled without cease near the well of the infinite Fall, between the abyss full of darkness, and the heavens. Suddenly a light beam from His prodigious eye, which formed the world from daylight, fell upon it. Beneath this shaft of soft and supernatural light, the feather quivered, shone, pulsated, grew, took shape, came alive, and seemed a splendor transformed into a woman. With the mysterious shifting of a soul, she arose, and, standing erect, lit infinity with her innocent smile. And the angels, trembling with love, beheld her. The twin cherubs clinging one to the other, the constellations of morning and evening, the Virtues, the Spirits, leaned forward to see this sister born of hell and of paradise. Never had the sacred heavens, amidst murmurs and whispers, contemplated a being more sublime. Seeing her both so proud and so pure, they hesitated between calling her eagle or virgin. Her face, melding flame with brilliance, blazed, defying the engulfing abyss; it was, beneath a charming brow, the glance of lightning with the eye of Dawn.

The archangel of the sun, gilded by a celestial fire, said:—O Lord, what shall we call this angel?—Then, in the Absolute where this Being dwells, one heard emerge from the depths of the Logos, this word which suddenly caused a star to blossom upon the brow of the magnificent, young angel, still half-formed and floating in the vast light:—Liberty.

20

"Her face, melding flame with brilliance, blazed,..."

"...the immense Hydra of darkness, opening its black wings."

Beyond the Earth III

I. SATAN IN THE NIGHT

I

I LOVE HIM!—NIGHT, SEPULCHRAL CELL, LIVING DEATH, darkness that my sombrous sob frightens, solitudes of evil where flees the great punished one, measureless glaciers of infinite winter, O torrents of dark chaos which saw me banished, despair whose cowardly peal of laughter I hear, void where Being, Time, Place, vanish, deep chasms, hells, abysses! I love God. I love him. That is all.—Light! Betrothed of all spirits; Sun! Fire of all thought; Life! Where art thou? I seek thee. O agony! Creation lives in a state of resplendence. O innocent glance of worshipped dawn, warmth with which nature is entirely imbued! Rivers are joyful amidst the grass; the horizon is aglow; the wind wanders; flowers fill the greensward; birds, birds, and more birds still. They all sing, laugh, love, flooded by the dawn. The tiger says:— What about me! I want my share of Heaven!—And so the dawn gilds the tiger and offers him to the Eternal.

I, alone, remain hideous! Alas! Nothing else is unclean. I, alone, am the shame and the stain of the world. My ugliness, vague terror of the anxious stars, pierces my night and so tarnishes the heavens. I see nothing, being cursed; but beyond, I hear, I hear in the water that flees, in the air that passes, I hear in the universe this murmur:—Go away!—The pig says to the dung-heap:—I despise Satan.—I sense the night thinking that I dishonor her. The whirling of the great sonorous breath, the morning wind, free and released into the sky, avoids my sad and pestilential brow.

Formerly, this daybreak, this innocent light, was I.—Me!—I was the archangel with the splendid brow, the fiery eye of the radiant azure, gilding the sky, life and Man; now I am the hideous star that bleaches the heap of bones. I once bore the torch, but I now drag the shroud. I arrive with night in hand; and everywhere I go, rearing up behind me, fully erect, is the immense Hydra of darkness, opening its black wings.

The boundless deeps retreat across their headlands. Everything before me, towards whom love once flew, recoils and flees. I was envious. That was my crime. All was said, and the sublime mouth cried:—Evil!—And God spat me into the abyss. Oh! I love him! That is the horror, that is the fire! What will become of me, abysses? I love God! I am damned!

II

Hell is eternal absence. Hell is loving. It is saying: Alas! So, where is she, my light? Where is my life and luminosity? She shows to bewildered glances her beauty. She smiles up there at others; others kiss her eyes, and upon her breast become inebriated and grow quiet; others possess her. Despair! Oh, when I was cast down from the height of splendor into this blindness, after the collapse of gloom upon my head, after the fall, naked, hurled from the summit forever, joined to the inexorable tomb, when I found myself alone at the bottom of infinity, I had a moment so dire that I began to laugh. The vast darkness filled me with its ecstasy, God was dying to me, and I felt in my heart the strange and wild plenitude of night. I shouted, joyful, triumphant, relentless:

—I declare war on these firmaments whose light is overwhelming, war on this heaven where God places so many false charms! He thought to chase me here, but it is I who escaped here. He believes me prisoner, but I am free. I soar. It is the Devil that is the eagle, and the world, the donkey. And I laugh. I am proud and happy. I left the vain, despicable, mean angels, and you, the Light who corrupts them, and you, Love, who suborns them! What a delight, this hatred, when it is boundless! This God, this heart of Everything, this radiant Father that the angel, the star, Man, and beast have within them, this heart around which the flock gathers, this Being, alone vital, alone true, alone necessary, that I am going to do without, me the punished colossus! It is good. How I shall curse this blessèd one! Whereas Adam praises him to the sky, I shall oppose him with insurrection, using my old power, and with flame, using the light rays I once possessed! How I shall roar at him! With what fervor I, the hideous one, shall confront, hate, execrate and loathe him, the supreme one.—and yet I love him!

IN THE AIR

Song of the Birds

Life! O joy! Deep woods,
    We are alive.
Endless flight entreats us;
Let us float upon the air, o'er the waters!
    Birds
Are made of soul-dust.

Come soar! Fly
    To the vales,
To the grottos, the shade, the places of respite!
Let us lose ourselves in this
    Ethereal sea
Where the cloud is an island!

From the heart of the rocks and rushes,
    From turrets,
From mounts that the day sets ablaze,
Let us fly, and, quivering, mad,
    Plunge
Into the indescribable ecstasy!

Fly, birds, to the bell-towers,
    To the promontories,
To the cliffs, the mountain peaks,
To the glaciers, lakes, and meadows;
    Savor
Your freedom from the abyss!

26

Life! azure! rays of light! thrills!
    Let us traverse
The vast, serene merriment,
Whilst high above the living,
    In the winds,
The shadow of the clouds trails close behind!

April flings wide open the gates
    Of spring;
Summer follows, and unfurls
Upon the earth a beautiful carpet
    Of wheat,
Of grasses, of flowers, of joy.

Let us drink, and eat; let us pick
    Festoons
From the bramble and vine;
The banquet in the forest
    Is ready;
Each branch is beckoning.

The peonies are on fire;
    The blue sky
Inflames a hundred blooming flowers;
The spring is, for our quite
    Delighted eyes,
A fiery furnace of roses.

You also gild us all,
    Fire so sweet that
Streams down from the heavens;

The eagles in flight are
    Flashes of lightning,
The sparrows, sparks.

We return to the light beams;
    We flee
To our mother limpidity;
The bird flies beyond the forest
    And appears
To vanish in the light.

Sometimes we move about the wheat,
    Overwhelmed;
But July has for resource
The shade, where, far from the warm furrows,
    We moisten
Our pink feet in the spring.

Since they lie beneath the heavens,
    Caring for
The happiness of the mead,
The grass and the hairy-tree
    Wished
In their tender reverie

That the fruits, the grain,
    The tranquil air,
The love-affair, the nest,
The dawn, the song, the allure,
    Should engage
Forever our timorous joy.

Let us live! Let us sing! Everything is pure
    In the blue;
Everything is beautiful in the light!
Everything towards its purpose, day and night,
    Is led;
Unerringly, the river meanders.

The whole countryside laughs;
    A spirit
Beats beneath each leaf.
—Let us love!—whispers a voice
    Within the woods;
And the flower wishes to be plucked.

When the iris has adorned
    The entire meadow,
When the warmer days increase,
When the evening glows in the
    Glittering pond,
When the greenery is lovely,

What says the dazzled gathering?
    Yes! yes! yes!
The hills, the fountains,
The green buds, the ripe fruit,
    The azures
Full of distant visions,

The field, the lake, the marsh,
    The cool cave,
Compose and, with neither tears nor sorrow,

Raise towards the eternal
        Heavens
This serene affirmation.

The dawn and the dazzlement
        Go on their way, sowing
Everywhere pearls of flame;
The bird is not an orphan;
        Everything is filled
With mysterious soul!

Someone unseen
        Is far away
In the unknown house;
And this stranger blesses
        Our nest,
And his window is the dawn.

And it is thanks to him
        That our wings
Never lack for support,
And that the doves go
        Onto the mountain
To drink where the gazelles drink.

Through this gentle unknown,
        Naked Adam
Smiled at us beneath the boughs;
The swan beneath the birch
        Finds water
To wash his white feathers.

30

Thanks to him, the woodpecker
        Lives free,
Darling of the venerable pines,
Delivering from ants
        His friends,
The cedars and maples.

Thanks to him, the sparrow
        From the elderberry
Flies up to the lofty elm;
It is he who creates the bush
        Wherein
We may sing and sleep.

He shelters us all,
        Hummingbird,
Goldfinch, wagtail,
The entire multitude delighted by the air
        And living
In the majestic blue glow.

Because of him, the breezes
        And the seas,
The stands of alders and holm-oaks,
The morning, the sage in flower,
        And the thyme,
Are radiant fêtes;

The wheat is golden, the skies
        Spacious,
The water joyful and the grass soft;

But he often gets angry
    When the wind
Steals from us our strands of moss.

He says to the wind:—Peace, south wind!
    And go!
Leave my birds alone.
Tear, if you will,
    The tresses
Of smoke from the dark cities!

The one beneath whom we soar
    Knows our names.
We sing. We are free of care.
Our humble, unwitting flight
    Is so great,
Our weakness so strong!

The storm, in thunderous flight,
    Unleashing
Waterspouts, hail, tumult,
Lashing, despite their tears,
    The large waves,
Is dulled by our frail feathers.

He wants the small creatures happy,
    The weather fine,
And innocence preserved;
He lowers, calm and gentle,
    As do we,
His wings o'er his brood.

"He wants the small creatures happy, the weather fine..."

Thanks to him, in the familiar
    Thicket, to which
Our wing is accustomed,
Upon velvet moss,
    Our loves
Are shed in the light.

He is good; and his goodness
    Is the summer;
It is the charming red rowen;
It causes nothing to befall us
    In our hollows
Without that the leaves stir.

His goodness is everything; it is the air,
    The clear flame,
The woods where, at evening dusk,
Your song, which takes flight,
    Nightingale,
Seems a dream of the moon.

It is what according to the seasons
    We do;
It is the rock which the water hollows;
It is the bird, lulled by the winds,
    Formed of
A happy inquietude.

He is powerful, star-studded,
    And veiled.
In the evening, with the murmurs

Of the flocks being escorted home,
    And the sound
Of bees beneath the blackberries,

With the darkness upon the roofs,
    Upon the forest,
Upon the near mountains,
It is his grandeur which descends,
    And which we feel
In the trembling of the oaks.

He had only to wish, one day,
    And love
Became the immense harmony;
All Beings were there;
    He mixed
His wisdom with their madness.

He wished that all be one;
    Perfume
Had for a sister the pure dawn;
And things, touching
    In a song,
Acquired a saintly nature.

He placed upon the deep waters
    Typhoons;
He set the flower upon its stem;
In large form he appeared
    Fulgurant;
The small was his miracle.

With the same beauty
    His lucidity
Created both the pleasing and the enormous;
He caused to emerge from the light beam
    The halcyon,
Which kisses the colossal sea.

The terrible became charming;
    The element,
Monster, giant, ghost,
Created by Him who wished
    It so,
Came to pair with the atom.

Then we saw in Ophir
    The humble asfir,
Green as the ferocious hydra;
And the blaze of Etna
    Shone
Upon the wing of the hummingbird.

Life is the sovereign and
    Serene word,
Without end, without form, without number,
Gentle, inexhaustible, ardent,
    O'erflowing
The entire dark earth.

Dawn marries dusk,
    The black beak
Mates with the flaming beak;

The flash of lightning, hideous male, pursues
      At night
The sea, his raucous female.

Let us fly, fly, fly!
      The furrows
Are plowed, and the wave is green.
Life is there before our eyes,
      In heaven,
Bright and fully revealed.

Swallow, make your nest.
      The granite
Offers you his shade and his ivy;
For your love, take turrets
      From the palace,
And straw from the humble cottage.

The nest which the bird builds
      So small
Is a profound thing;
The egg removed from the forest
      Would
Unbalance the world.

III

If I did not love him, I would not suffer. Let me reascend, abysses!....—But no! step by step I fall, I sink, at each effort I slip further. The curse of the night, his means of torture, is to worship daylight but to remain in the dark. This love is sinister, and

37

"Unable to rise up, even when I desire it!"

evil is its fruit. O my light, where art thou? Satan implores you. Do you hear me? Speak. Return, dawn, dawn, dawn! Do not tell them: forever; and me: never! I suffer!—Oh! everything is black, I do not see, I hate!

I hate!—Yes, I hate you, human heap, bloodless crowd, because you love him, because God loves you, because his light sparkles through your bones, because you immerse your urns in his streams, because you pass, living, into nature, because, while torture torments me, and I have, for vulture, my own soul, you have hope in your eyes and love in your hearts!

Men, larvae, nothingnesses, shadows, harried faces, you are unhappy! O foolish, chosen ones, you complain of aging every day, of fading away, of sensing your blood growing cold, and you accuse God! How fanciful you are! I have lost more than you! I have seen fall, one after the other, my beams of light, and you, merely your hair!

IV

Unable to rise up, even when I desire it! What! Repentant souls fly up from their tombs, radiant. Owls become doves. Demons, forgiven, return to the firmament; and I, abject specter, see them slowly turning white in the dismal night, again becoming angels! Stars, those flowers of the abyss, bloom in the mires! What! Caesar has departed! Torquemada gone away! Busiris, within the cavern where Jehovah holds him, discerns a light and begins to smile! Nimrod is waiting. I have just heard Judas say, in the gaol where his crime and I bind him:—I now have no more than four million centuries left, chained in the darkness.—

How happy Judas is! He can count. For all, for everyone, daylight will reappear. Cain, even agèd Cain himself, will depart!

Whereas I, alone, shall remain in the mournful deserts. Bottomless horror! I am lord of the shades. I shall remain wretched, forever.

V

But I shall take revenge upon his humanity, upon Man whom he created, upon Adam and Eve, upon the smiling soul, upon the breaking day, upon you, star! upon you, wing! you, flower! Upon the virgin, and the mother, and upon the child! Woe unto you! I shall deform the universal countenance.

Being serpent, I shall shake my rattle in the darkness. I shall invent gods, Moloch, Vishnu, Baal. I shall use the real to crush the ideal, stones of edens to build sodoms. Through the branches of the forest of men will be seen my gleaming eyes, and it shall be said: It is he. More afraid of evil than inspired by good, the wise shall doubt God. I shall bite the soul. I shall make love unseemly in the hearts of women. I shall mix my cinders with these dying coals, and, evil, I shall laugh, scratching out all their instincts and all their virtues with the talons of my wings. I shall be so hideous that all eyes shall possess some indefinable darkness; and the vile and the perverse shall grow like field grass. The son shall appear before the indignant judge, holding handfuls of white hair from his butchered father. I shall say to the poor: Steal; to the rich: Oppress. I shall make mothers cast their newborn into latrines. Tremble, O God! I shall open their breasts with my hands, I shall tear away their steaming hearts and wring from them all crime, horror, betrayal, murder, Achab, Tiberius, Atreus, onto your radiant and sacred creation!

You shall be Providence and I, Fate. Better than creating hatred, O emptiness! O blindness! I have created envy. In vain does benevolent God propagate these giants whose soul is full

"Being serpent, I shall shake my rattle in the darkness."

of light beams: genius, love, and heroism. Through denial, I eat away at faith. I am Zoilus. Around Socrates, I call forth Anytus, and place Thersites in the presence of Achilles. And all weep; and I make equal, by means of poisons, the bloating of dwarfs and the splendor of Titans. Matter has my sign upon her brow. I quarrel with her. I frighten fathomless water beneath abysses of hail. I compel the ocean and earth, which God keeps under his rule, to create chaos with me. I fashion enormous deformity with their powers, a beast out of spume, a monster out of crust, Leviathan upon the sea, Behemoth upon the earth. Everywhere do I complete chaos through Hell, the ogre through the idol, and rats, weasels, the torpedo, the hyena tearing at skeletons, the slaver of the toad, the tooth of the crocodile, through the bonze, the obi, the fakir, and the imam.

God passes through the hearts of men, but I remain there. His wheel rolls and turns with a sidereal sound, but it is my dismal and bloody grain that it grinds. A recoiling Jehovah now senses, everywhere, a creation of Satan beneath his own. His fire cannot flame without that my breath appear. He is the chariot, and I the rut. Our forces overlap, and I use his pure, innocent sun to create plagues, poisons, monsters, deserts. It is God who creates the brow, and I the care engraved upon it. He is in the prophet and I in the soothsayer. War and grief! I take from him all his divine swords—the sword of air: wind, the sword of water: rain, lightning's sword, the bewilderment of the dazzled earth—and I make terrible use of them. And nature is afraid. From my breath, a hydra hatches in the vapor, and the drop of water swells into a mighty torrent. With the bright hearth that warms, I set ablaze. I make from honey, gall, from the harbor, the reef. God blesses the best, I anoint the strongest. God creates the radiant, and I the bloodthirsty.

42

Yes, to crush his children I shall take his thunderbolts! Yes, I shall draw myself up to my full height! I wish to slay this creator in all that he creates. I wish to torture him in his work, and to hear his death rattle amidst justice and decency corrupted, in the fields that war crushes with its bounding, in the peoples delivered up to tyrants, in good folk and in saints, in the entire human soul! I want that he struggle, spirit beneath matter, that he bleed in the murdered, just man. I want that he writhe, covered with monstrous priests, that he weep, gagged by idolatries. I want that lilies die and roses wither, that from the swan quivering beneath the beaks of vultures, from the beauties, the virtues, from everywhere, his blood, his own divine blood, flow upon him and drown him.

Behold! Look, heavens! The scaffold is the world. I am the dark executioner, and I execute God. God shall die. Thanks to me, the chariots beneath their axles, kings with their power, the eagles with their claws, sinister, obscure dogmas from pontiffs, all that stand upon earth at this time, even the innocent, shall have something of God that they will crush beneath their feet in the darkness. My flames, creeping beneath the universe, shall set him ablaze.

I am evil; I am night; I am terror.

VI

Have mercy! Forgive me! Summon me back! Make away with me! Have mercy! Should not all chains be broken, all evil end, and all hatred be extinguished, disappearing amidst your serenity? What! The good is infinite, evil is without limit! You the good, I the evil! Is it possible? The world governed by an invis-

"I wish to slay this creator in all that he creates."

ible pair! Of what are you thinking, Lord? A sharing between us! No, you are the countenance, and I the knees. Let me bend and drop, immense Master, onto this bedrock of Heaven called Clemency!

Have mercy, O God! The universe, the lands and waters, the boundless azure full of invisible birds, the glaucous oceans which roar out their waves, the living enormity whence shine the worlds. What! It is a balance on which we both bear weight! What say you, suns? He charming, I hideous! What! He on one scale, suns, and I on the other! The flesh is my handmaid and the soul is his apostle. I struggle. We each take sides. To be infinite, is to be equal. Your paradise simply balances my prison. Ah! Creation presses down upon me like a mountain. I raise my brow through the chaos whence my pains fall again as plagues. I writhe without respite, without end, without hope.

It is a majesty, such suffering. Yes, it is the enigma, O night, of your millions of eyes: the great sufferer faces the great mysterious one. Have mercy, O God! For you, yourself, I must obtain it. My eternity casts darkness upon yours. Before your eye-torch nothing must remain, everything must change, grow old, and be transformed. You alone exist. Before you all must age. And, for your grandeur, it is an unwelcome cloud, this specter that one can see seated at the heart of your azure heaven, eternal Satan sitting before eternal God!

VII

They are up there, on high! They are amidst the hymn and the jubilation. The æther of paradise unfolds before them. They soar happy, caring, earnest, within the brilliance of mysterious heaven. Their robes in the azure make folds of light. They are in

45

"...and I dream as I lean upon this deep tomb."

their first innocent and pure state. They go from one world to the other as do the birds. Love bends them as the wind does the reeds, and again uplifts them as the hearth lifts its flames. They are engulfed in God while remaining souls, and contemplate, happy, the face of illumination. They mate, flooded in bliss. They watch him be, he watches them live. They rise forever towards him. He intoxicates them with the unheard-of smile of his vastness. He sees them. He speaks to them. He is Grace and Beauty. The impenetrable is gentle, the formidable is tender...

—Oh! I should like to seize, to tear away, to hold, to capture, Oh! I should like to crush the morning star!

The lame, the leprous, and the hesitant blind, those who walk unshod, and those who have no shelter from the cold, they are rich. God loves them. They have for raiment your kind-hearted gaze. God! To be unloved, that is nakedness! To be accursed is pitch and brimstone.

VIII

I placed beneath a stone and sealed within a chasm, justice, goodness, purity, truth, beauty. All that could serve Man as a torch: virtue, reason, thought, hope, belief, that which is called wisdom, and that which is called glory, and I dream as I lean upon this deep tomb. I am immense. And beneath me the darkness uncreates what the light has created; and in the black abysses, brooding, I hear crimes accruing drop by drop. Chaos contemplates me, and I tread on him. Alas! Alas! Better the stable where Jesus was born than Babel and Nineveh and Tyre and Babylon, and better Job on his dunghill than Satan upon his throne!

Oh! If I were happy, I would be good! Pity! I would not invoke malediction! Did the wild ass bray, did the ox bellow

"Kill! Strike! Condemn! I am scared! I am cold!"

while grazing happily in their fields? Love, the azure, the lilies, the magnificent light, the great golden rays that lengthen as they pass, the virgins, the joyful children, the innocent angel, the golden fringe of dawn at the edges of ravines, Oh, I shout desperately toward these divine things that I can no longer see!—God! God!—The splendors of heaven, alas, add more of night to my prison. Howls fall upon me from all the harmonies. Torture! I wish to touch the thick clouds, I reach out to the flowers, I shout to the north winds: Forgive me! Having all the ills of the world for rags and tatters, I weep, I ask the bramble, the wheat, the cloud, the tomb, the star, the blade of grass, the animals recoiling before the human countenance, the stones which the convict breaks beside the road, everything, the day which dawns, the wind which blows anew, from them all, I ask for pity! I am the immense beggar.

IX

Still, if I could sleep! If only for an hour, a minute, an instant, one moment, the time that a wave spends on a sonorous lakebed, could I but lay my brow upon some hard and funereal bedside, even to wake up more lamentable! If I could, naked, on a block of bronze or on a pile of stones, one or the other, alas! but close my eyes, and stretch out, and feel something fresh, soft and serene, as if I died! If I could but lose myself for a moment in a dream, soothe in my side what is restless and wearing, inhale a strange, ærial, impalpable fluid, and float, hearing nothing, neither my flapping wing, nor my beating heart, nor these shouts on earth of which I am the cause:—Kill! Strike! Condemn! I am scared! I am cold! I am hungry!—sensing my miserable ear deaf at last!

Oh! To lie down, to place my talons under my head, to say:—It is good! I sleep, just like any other beast, like a leopard, a jackal, a wolf! An august, calm cloud dissolves me!—But no! Never! I drag insomnia along, forever, in a sinister vastness of agony. To not die, to not sleep. This is my fate. In a dream, one does not vanish, but it is believed that one does so, that is enough. I have no such respite. My punishment is to be here, still standing; to be an eternal hatred, watching fearfully in the dark, my eye evermore fixed upon black cliffs of unfathomable mystery. To see always fleeing, as an unattainable isle, sleep and dream, the vague, blue paradises where smiles some indescribable, misty azure! O condemnation!

I remain beneath this vault. I regard the profound horror, and I heed it. No being can suffer without that I am there. I am the hideous sphere of sorrows, and feel each pulsation of the world's fever. My hearing is the point of confluence where is repeated and muttered all the sinister sounds in the sparse expanse. I hear the darkness. O agony! Evil from far and near brings to my prison its mournful, bitter joy. I hear the asp slither and the hemlock grow. Evil from the zenith to the nadir presses down upon me. The sea may well squall, the avalanche rumble, the storm appear, to hurl down thunderbolts, the brilliant zodiac may well turn its wheel of constellations, dark millstone of the heavens, through the enormous and prodigious roar of the stars whose vast cluster sometimes cants—through the ocean, the lightning, and the avalanche rolling from the mountain heights amidst the green pines, I still hear the tread of a lone crime at the far end of the universe. I discern everything: the whispered word, which is false, the dark thrill of the wheat that embraces the tares, the gangrene that comes to bite the open wound, the voiceless murmur of the waves flooding the

"I regard the profound horror, and I heed it."

skiff, the silence of the dog near the thrush's nest, I can escape nothing, and everything befalls me, at once, in this prison where I am submerged.

All plagues resound within me; and I feel the consequence of every monster. I dream, listening to the fury, the fall, the lie of this entire squalid race of Japheth. I even distinguish the mysterious sound made by a heinous crime planned within a conscience. O night! I hear Nero become a parricide.

Sleep, darksome abode, ineffable space, where one is soft as the dawn and pure as the newborn child! To sleep, O healing, detachment, dew, stupor in full bloom, immense, soothèd shadow, sacred repose, silent tenderness, a lulling, dark and charming, which steeps the hearts in the heavens, Oh! this bath for remorse, this balm for ulcers, the peace which is releasing what was caught in the claw, to never have that! Never! Never to have this slumber on hazy summits, this sleep, before whom souls are the same, which transforms the lair into a nest, and permits bees to fly in the open mouths of lions! Oh! this voice which says:—Let us become calm and unfettered!—To never hear it in my convulsive nights! The enflamed eyes and the slavering gums, to stay awake, awake, to gnash one's teeth, those are the depths to which my fault has sealed me! Hideous fate! To lock me in Night, and deprive me of sleep! To deliver me unto this pungent burning, vigil without repose, the regard always dire, always open! O pitiless night! To be unable to take from it a little peace, and have it entirely enwrap me! Sunk in oblivion, to not taste a drop of it! To always be watchful! Always on the alert!

O all you Beings! Sons of darkness or of sunlight, whoever you may be, dead, living, birds of the Ærial spirits, specters of day, embryos of dreams, faces of the invisible, angels, ghosts,

"...soothèd shadow, sacred repose, silent tenderness..."

come, you shall find Satan with eyes open. Soar, crawl, depart, return: Satan watches with eyes open. Be it darkness or rose-ate dawn, his eyes are open. Yesterday, tomorrow, forever! Let flee the treads of time, be they sluggish or brief, after millions of days, months, years, centuries, seasons born or fading, ebbs and flows, springs and winters, come, you shall find Satan with eyes open! Two fixed eyes, that is the very nadir of terror. The ghostly, unformed, deceitful, chimerical darkness keeps me in these chasms, gaping and burdened by the monstrous weight of Nothingness. I suffer. Oh! Would that I could sleep, if but for an instant!

X

I love him for being beautiful, I, who am so deformed. For one moment, let me forget!—O memory!—I see the angels whispering with him in the dark. What does he say to them? I am jealous! I remember that he once spoke with me, that the light was beautiful. I love him for being good, I who am evil. Oh! If, for the length of a lightning flash, alas! I could but see his shadow appear, here at the bottom of my chaos! I adore him, this God, more than Jephthah his priest, more than Amos his prophet and David his singer. I love him for being honest, I who am a liar. Blood burns my eyes, foam fills my mouth, and, dog of infinity, driven from Heaven, fierce, wild, crying for my master at the threshold of day, chewing upon the human race, I howl out my love! Yes, dog!

While speaking of him, my voice becomes horrible. Sometimes, feeling pensive, stooped beneath my terrible vault, I hear the seraphim singing of him in the heavens, and, when they are through, the echo sings after them. Then I say:—Well, I also, like

54

they, God, wish to sing of you; O light, I love thee! I wish, with an infernal song, to delight the echo of Heaven. Satan is a lyre as well as Gabriel. God! it is of you, true day, it is of you, sole refuge; God! it is of you, shepherd, king, father, teacher, judge, that creation dreams eternally! And foolish, old heart of iron attracted by the magnet, I say:—Glory!—And my strophe bursts out into a crown, and I sing an ineffable and supreme hymn, a hymn of charming verses filled with darkness and ecstasy, and which could have come from the mouth of a lily...

Then I listen; and the echo that answers me barks!

XI

Even the gloomiest prisons have a clerestory. At the bottom of the dungeon, at the bottom of the hutch, something still seems to exist; here, nothing. Satan turns towards Jehovah, weary of the abyss. Oh! I am the sole murderer and the sole victim. I have for torment only the evil that my own hands create. Other beings exist, and then are no more; they move, then stop; a sound, then nothing. I envy them. They are dead, whereas I am widowed of Life. I am the frightful living being of the tomb.

Yes, the tortured one howls and emits the death rattle. The law holds him in dreadful irons, kills him slowly, butchers him bit by bit, and sometimes pauses, that the dying might be prolonged. His feet smoke, his flesh crackles, and at times flames, and we see the entrails from his stomach. He screams; the oil boils in the vat. Tongs, molten lead, the wheel, horror! By degrees, however, despite the vile and increasingly ardent torturer, the torture is wasted on an unconscious man. Grim agony arrives, dreadful, gentle. Vanquished torment seems to wander about the surface; and the sufferer, at the time of dying, feels

"They are dead, whereas I am widowed of Life."

a mysterious estrangement from the torture. From between his burnt lashes a dim light slips away. It is death, it is heaven, it is deep infinity. He sinks there, he drifts there, he feels himself dissolving: his open eyes become fixed on the void. He is dead! Oh! that, abysses, is what I so desire. I crave it, and I shout:—Help me, executioners!—The wheel with the thousand teeth, the rack, the hooks, the attentions of the frightful, deliberate and barbaric judge, pincers, red hot clamps, blows with iron bars, the burning oil eating away at the granite vat, the iron, the fire, it is good, it is gentle, it bestows an end.

XII

Have pity, abysses, prison, Gehenna, tomb, chaos, night, desolation, hatred, have pity, if Heaven will not! on Satan, fallen so low from such heights. O vaults of Hell, let your tears flow! No, it is God, it is Heaven, it is the azure full of charms, the dawn surrendering herself fully revealed to my eyes, it is the kiss of day, it is love that I desire! But I have nothing, only mourning. Nothing but winter! Nothing but bitter solitude! Vile chaos, always in the same posture! Mysterious masses of expiation! I may not even, alas! see a vision, or the subdued light one can see in the daytime through a sieve. I hear the horrible monologue of nothingness, and the unlimitedness for me contains only insult. Never God! Everything is black. When my hand seeks, upon my brow, the two light beams of the archangel, it only finds there the two horns of the billy goat; I do not know what she-wolf holds existence in her mouth, carries it off and bites it, and comes to lick me in the darkness, saying:—I am death.—What! Must despair be my eternal dwelling! Horror! I love thee, O God! Forgive me, O my God!

Indeed, do weep. Sob, beseech, foam with rage, love! and be rebuffed! Always repeat the same baseness! Dog Satan, wallow eternally in your lowliness!—Oh; I rise up and descend and rise again unceasingly, searching the cavern of creation; the base is steel, the ceiling, bronze, forever, and ever, and ever! I shudder, and I seek, I shout, and I call. No one! And furious, trembling, desperate, banished, striking the infinite with my feet, hands, and brow, as a gnat strikes a dark windowpane, tearing patches of shadow from the mournful vastness, alone, finding no exit, sightless, in the night, I grope along this wall: Eternity.

XIII

—Here is the tomb, and there, chaos; overhead, blackness, beneath my feet, the Fall. Where I stop, the deep collapses upon itself, and everything is empty. Well, all these abysses mingled above me would be nothing were I, myself, to alter my thought, were I able to revel in my pent-up fury, and persuade myself that I hate! It is not the stupefied, voiceless crypt of doom, it is not the prison, the pit, the Gehenna, it is neither the lock, nor the chain, it is one's own heart that holds one captive. To hate brings deliverance.

XIV

Alas, through too much abnegation, and by sinking my bitter blade, derision, into everything, by mocking the great nuptial poems, and shouting in the depths at crimes:—I am with you!— and by perpetuating Nimrod in Attila, and Caiaphas in Borgia, by dint of adding to every wing a claw, by inspiring the lowliest deeds and casting my cesspool into the beams of light, by being the infamous angel steeped in every crime possible in dark nature, and by saturating myself with darkness, I become cold.

XV

Oh! God's essence is to love. Man believes that God is, like him, merely a soul, and that he absents himself from the universe, an immense cloud of dust taking wing. But I, sad enemy and eternal mocker, I know this: God is not a soul, but is a heart. God, loving center of the world, to his divine fibers attaches all the rootlets of all the roots, and his tenderness is the same for the worm as for the seraph. The endless expanses are astonished that this appalling heart, blasphemed by the priests, has as many light beams as the universe has beings. For him, to create, think, meditate, bring to life, to sow, to destroy, to make, to be, to see—is but to love. Magnificent, he loves, and in natural response his creatures worship him. Everything permeates him; he prizes the night through the dawn, the spirits through the idea, flowers through their scent. And this heart in its abyss has everything,—except one. Except Satan, forever rejected, damned, mournful. God excludes me. He ends with me. I am God's outermost limit, and he would be infinite were I not to exist.

I say to him:—You did well, God, when you struck me down!—I by no means accuse him, no! But I despair! O somber eternity, I am the son without a father. In regard to Satan, he exists, but is no longer God.

XVI

A hundred times, a hundred times over, I repeat the confession: I love! And God tortures me; and here is my blasphemy, here my frenzy and my howling: I love! I love, enough to make the heavens tremble!—But! It is in vain! Oh! What is incredible, what is horrible, what is divine, is to rise up, opening senseless wings, clinging, blood-stained, to every thought that one can seize, with cries, with tears, sounding the terrors, probing the pains, all those that one suffers and all those that one invents, traversing the entire range of dismay, only to fall again into the same despair!

God wants that the tired man sleep, so he creates the evening. He digs for the mole a burrow; he grants the monkey, the bear, the lynx, the panther, the harsh haven of caverns and mountains. For the whales he provides the seas, for the toads, the silt, and to the serpents shaking their rattles, he proffers reeds. He causes planets to revolve about their suns and spindles to revolve in the pure hands of virgins. He enters nests, touches the fledglings, and says:—The north wind is coming, I shall thicken their feathers.—He lets the spark fly off from the anvils, and allows it to escape the hammers, joyful. He shows his grand heavens to the lions of Athos. He displays, in the dawn, the springs full of bees, as well as flowerbeds beneath floods of light beams. His pride in the world is transformed into kindness. A vast burning light sets everything ablaze, from the archangel to the brute and from the star to the stone. It intersects in the forest of fire its branches of light, goes, comes, falls, fecundates, inflames, fills, fights Winter who binds rivers to their beds, making Winter release them, and laughs in all matters, gleaming softly behind a rose leaf, glittering, and warming the sidereal enormity of the heavens. But, for me, monstrous prodigy, this blaze rears up in a wall of ice! Yes, happy creation completely intertwines light and mist, spirit and body, within this good Lord, forming unspeakable harmony. The most defiled being again finds innocence in his very tenderness and omnipotence. I alone, I the cursed, the incurable apostate, I approach God with no result other than to cause faint, rumbling thunder!

God wishes that this swarm of atoms venerate him. He demands of them their heart, their song, their fruit, their perfume, their prayer—from me, nothing, night. O bottomless misery! Hear this, spheres, stars, firmaments, O ancient suns, my brothers, towards whom my dolorous desire rises, weeping, O heavens, azures, depths, splendors—Love hates me!

II. THE ANGEL LIBERTY

I

Light. And then more light still. Chaos of constellations in the abysses of dawn. The angel Liberty soars in the spacious azure. It seems that she is looking for a way out of Heaven. She sees a star, and approaches:—Listen, Star; lead me beneath the fatal vault. God permits me to talk to him who was once great.—I cannot—answers the celestial body. And Liberty continues:— At least tell me where, and how I may descend.—Speak to the Lightning—says the star. He alone can tell you. He, alone, of Heaven's angels, knows how to fall.—And the angel Liberty, on wings over which even the wind has no say, left, and crossed the dark æther.

Her flight was eternal—Man has no number with which to measure the time—and was proud and sure. Suddenly, in a formless corner of the azure, she spied the huge stable of thick clouds. One could hear the sound of loose chains, and of we know not what terrible axles turning. The angel Lightning, at

"Light. And then more light still."

work in this, one of the Heavenly Caverns, was releasing all the chariots of thunder, some composed of common flame, others as if forged in Hell by the nights. And incredible streamings of lightning traced vaguely their dreadful shapes. The reefs in the sea, the bulls in the stable, make mere cooings beside the monstrous din of all these chariots forged in the abyss.

Liberty advanced toward the angel Lightning. She, the Immortal one, smiled, and spoke:—Angel, you must know brilliant Lucifer, fallen to his doom. —It is I who struck him down, yet I know him not, says Lightning.—But to the abyss where you cast this soul, can you guide me?—No, says the spirit of flame. Go seek out the old angel Winter. He, alone, knows the dark folds of the shroud. I, however, remember nothing. I merely strike, and pass on.—Then he pointed to a black speck in space. It was the earth. —Go, he says. Sad Hell borders on this world, and there you shall find Winter.—

And the angel Liberty, taking wing like a catapult shot, watched the dark, round sphere growing near, and, magnificent, braving the north wind and the mistral, landed on the earth in the sepulchral place. In this frightful circle enclosed by glaciers, at the bottom of the ghastly desert where never passed Columbuses or da Gamas, those luminous probers, in this darkness and in these depths conquered by Nothingness upon their creation, beyond the Spitzbergs, the floods and ice floes, in the center of the mist where light beams end, far from day, in the marble water, in the granite sea, the somber archangel, Winter, draws himself up upon the Pole—the trumpet at his mouth and the shadow upon his shoulder, forever there, in the midst of this bereavement; from his clarion a breath, a lightning flash from his eye. Never does he even dream, being composed of snow. The wingèd winds, resembling trapped birds, are enclosed within his

63

hand, captives of the eternal silence. His blear eye looks hideously at the sky, the hoarfrost in his bones, the hoarfrost upon his head. Petrified horror comes to rest about him; and his sinister bearing frightens the Infinite. Hard, dismal, he is ice-bound, that is to say, banished. The earth beneath his feet, clad in darkness, keeps silent; he is the white and mute statue standing upon this tomb in eternal night.

Nary a light, a movement, a sound, touch this giant, alone as he is beneath somber veils. But when, upon these dials that we call stars, the hour of the last day without end and without middle chimes, the light shining from God's countenance shall thaw this specter, of a sudden his mouth shall swell with a formidable, fierce fold, and the worlds, those aimless, oarless skiffs, shall hear the hurricane burst forth from his clarion. Never does the seraph spangled with stars approach this soul of silence and mourning, turned to stone, gaoler of the dead heavens and the black firmaments. This grey fog, like eventide, frightens the rapturous and tender cherubs. The snows, that horrifying body of ash, make of this horizon whose verge is scorned by Dawn, something like the inside of a crypt.

The Angel-virgin, across the glaciers, those white ruins, flew straight towards the giant, alone in these dark deserts that Day desires not, nor does it recognize. At first she glided, radiant, above the menacing colossus, with the great circling of the eagle. Then, upon approaching, she spoke:—The One who judges and rules, the One who makes everything live and who makes everything tremble, allowed me to come. I wish to speak to a frightening Being whose cave only you know. O giant, open the abyss for me, so that I may enter—The Old Man of the Night remained deaf and mute; hardly a fold of the heavy fog did stir in this immensity of darkness and solitude. Yet, with nothing appearing

"...gaoler of the dead heavens and the black firmaments."

"...two walls without form whence smoke was rising,..."

to disturb him, and with no movement showing he had heard, the ice beneath his feet slowly began to crack. A strange fissure appeared, opening above an unknown and no longer natural horror, the mouth of a pale and gloomy well, a steep slope of a chasm leading towards the beyond, a vision of a formidable nothingness enclosed between two walls without form whence smoke was rising, mourning, mist, fathomless darkness without contour. The virgin Liberty, pure and composed of daylight, felt the cold from this disastrous place where nothing exists. The desolation of this abyss was mournful and profound; and it was endless night. She opened her great wings where the blue of the Heavens shines, and calmly descended into this terrible darkness.

II

Now, at this very moment, the inseparable horror, without palpitation, breathless and echoless, the sorrowful union of tomb and chaos that we call Hell, saw something extraordinary. A form, sometimes suddenly vanishing, then reappearing, floating far off, then engulfed, a kind of veil stirring uncertainly, dropped beneath this ceiling which we would take for a dream. This figure seemed like what the bank of the river Seine had seen wandering in days of old, casting into the winds its formidable voice. She wandered, as seaweed wanders. Through the veil the fixedness of her eyes blazed, and the cloth of which this veil was composed seemed to have been woven of dream and darkness. She sounded the hell that stretches on forever. In this stagnation of gloom, which dreams, and has the fierce air of a voiceless crime, she made a pass, turned, descended, reascended, taking who knows what formless folds for guides, here pale in dark places, there dark in pale places. Thus does the kestrel fly amidst the branches of trees. Sometimes, as someone searching, she touched the prodigious wall of the vault of the world. She meandered, slow and supple as a wave, in the abyss where the spirit reads this mournful word: Absent. And she often left behind, in passing, the fleeting, pale blue stain of sulphur.

But suddenly sensing more abyss beneath her, she paused, tilted her head, and looked. The night no day interrupts lay in that terrible and sublime expanse. This precipice was a chasm composed of Death, and one sensed the dissolved sepulcher floating there. One could see night beneath night; below the darkness, in that strange space, could be seen more darkness. Right at the very bottom moved a dark shape; this glimpsed ghost, immersed, troubled, fleeing, wandering, crawling, was He, the Accursed. One could see his forehead, his wings, his spine. It was the archangel specter, soul of the funereal places, mixing celestial body with beast. It was the sinister Being in whom Evil thinks. It was the criminal executed by Crime. It was more than a fallen soul. It was the Fall.

Chaos turned over upon the angel, and swelled up within him. At times a talon, a wide skull, a flank crossed with lines like lynxes, wasps and zebras, rose up in the horrible spasm of darkness. Its scales looking jet black and made of smoke, it seemed like one of those vague, meandering, floating things whose sting we fear. Offering all of its aspects in a lurid sketch, celestial, bestial, human, vertigonous, letting show one face in the midst of its coils, swelling with confused folds in the gloom where nothing shines, it was at times hydra and sometimes larva. It dragged itself along, viscous, pallid, eclipsed, soiled, colossal reptile of the infinite cesspool. The nethermost cavern of Everything—that was this abyss. It was space in tears, and miasma that suffers. Hideous rocks prefigured black

"...she paused, tilted her head, and looked."

"...its aspects in a lurid sketch, celestial, bestial, human, vertiginous,..."

emaciations. At times one believed that one glimpsed, in the thick mist, the terrible corpse of Cause. Everything was dead. Satan was prowling about in some formless and hideous place which seemed destroyed, so that in the midst of fetid night, everything being blackness, plague, terror, suffering, lividity, ruin, it seemed destined that, in the depths of this grave, this crawling worm would be seen.

If some angel, wandering in eternal winter, searching the depths of impenetrable bereavement, alas, happened upon this wretch, he would find nothing, in this king of Hell, of the enlightened giant once called Lucifer. The abyss had finally absorbed him. The condemnation—heavy, leprous, enormous—had, upon this forever rejected archangel, slowly been deposited as monstrosity. Impure typhoid was on his bitter breath. Sometimes, in this dark well filled with chimeras that the imagination alone sees and understands, some streaming of light traced his back or the foul membrane of his wing. The roundness of his red, glistening eye seemed, in the terror of these incredible places, a drop of flame deep in the wells of night. His face was the frightened mask of vertigo.

At certain times, phases of this prodigious gloom, a blazing fire escaped from him, engulfing him; the blind abyss was suddenly luminous. Then, dark vision! through the fathomless, through the unknown that is not watchable, in the strange depths of the chasm become sea-green around the unspeakable and naked giant, Satan appeared in all his suffering. The fulgurant devil, frightful in this translucence, writhed like drowned lightning. Then came back the night, icy and merciless. The vast cecity flowed back beneath the vault of eternal silence and swallowed him whole, and Hell, revealed for but a moment, closed again, mournful, fading away into blackness.

VII

Everything was silent at the bottom of the ebbless gulf, and dead immobility was disturbed no more. Like seaweed that the waters support and lull, Satan still slept. In the cover of night where sank his body built of fancy, what one glimpsed was his human form. Like the white snowflake carried by a winter wind, the angel stopped upon her floating wings, and wept. Her tears seemed tears of light flowing from two stars. Like the tarantula amidst its webbing, the great wretched and wicked one was palpitating; and the immortal virgin, tilting the lit carbuncle atop her head, stretched her arms towards the angel engulfed within the beast, and spoke, hovering, and yet still upon her knees. And the tone of her divine voice was softer than the faint, dark incarnation of the spheres:

—O Thou; I come. I weep. Here, in the miseries, in mourning, in the Hell where starlight has disappeared, I come to beseech you, O cursed one! Here, I am no more than a glistening tear. What survives of you is me. I am your daughter. Do you sense my presence? Tell me, do you recognize me? Do you hear me? It is from the depths of the divine paradises, it is from the bright and sacred deep, it is from that great, lucent heaven where lives the One who creates, that I come, desperate, to you, the angel buried! I cried out to God; and formidable God said: Yes. He lets me descend to the bottom of the deformed nights, and, so that I may speak to you, he lets you sleep. Because, Father, for your eyes, alas! the firmament can half-open only in dream!

Oh! All this darkness is hideous! Father, Father! What! You in this dungeon! What! You in this lair! You punished, you evil, you, the eldest son of the elect! You here, thus, so low that God no longer sees you! Hell! Ocean of Night! No wave, no

"Oh! All this darkness is hideous! Father, Father!"

spume, no wind. Everywhere Blackness. It is, in the mist, your
sorrowful breath that I hear. The length of your mourning shall
exceed Time; the amount of your troubles shall exceed Number.
The Suns said to me:—Take care, he is in the darkness!—But
I said:—I must see this desperate being.—Alas, the star in the
sky abhors you, the flower in the meadow fears you, around you
all the beings together shudder, brightness quivers, the azure
trembles, infinity dreads you and loathes you; well, I nonetheless
bring you, with love, all this immense dismay!

I come to beseech you in your exile. In your tarnished state,
I come to bathe you in tears. I make Light kneel down before
your horror, and I make Hope kneel down before the lightning
strikes imprinted upon your black brow! Hear me in your dream
through the anathema. Be not angry, father, because I love you!
The wounded person does not hate the hand that supports
him. The starving man has never cursed the one who arrives,

saying:—Here is some bread and here, some water; drink and eat.—Oh! When I was still amongst your feathers, what an angel Satan was, in the dawn and in the immensity! God naming himself Goodness, you were named Beauty. Your hair was fair and preternatural, it quivered magnificently, and left behind it a flood of light rays in the night! The abyss was governed by you as well as by God.

One day, the elements took you for him. As you raised yourself up with your diadem into the heavens flooded by your frightening sheen, the breeze said:—Emmanuel!—and the wave:—Adonai!—Your chariot made worlds spring up beneath its wheels. Next to you, Raphael, Gabriel, whose brow sheds a meteor scattered in flames, Michael, whose light never ceases, Ithuriel, who combines light beams with solaces, Stellial, Azrael, torchbearer of souls, were no more than confused creatures inhabiting the forest. A brilliance of whiteness surrounded you; and the dawn upon seeing you exclaimed:—I am dark!—You passed by in a storm of glory. The æthers awaited you, that they might become azures. Universes were born, prodigious and pure, with millions of flowers and fulgurations, in a rhythm marked by the beating of your wings. You made, by fixing on them your charming eye, the suns draw back in resplendence. You glowed, innocence and strength; a lily archangel! Just as, behind the hero, marches the phalanx, so, in your retinue, walked the constellations. The darkness wept with love when we traversed her. At night, you rose up in a triumphal procession of stars; and the divine vaults and the sacred pilasters, and the eternal heavens and the newborn Eden, adored you in your immense joy, unfortunate one!

Alas, as soon as you were cast down into this prison, where no glance enters, you created this dream, in order to avenge yourself, giant demon, on Infinity! Near the exiled angel you placed ban-

"You created in the nether regions, with your miasmas, demons."

"...growing ever larger, the enormous sword in the shape of a cross."

ished Man. You brought down Adam and you made Eve fall. You wished to strike God in the bud and the sap, in the child, in the nest amongst the trees, in the halcyon. Alone, walled up forever beneath Creation, you became, in horror, the great disastrous dreamer. In the virgin forests you made the plague emerge from the delightful and astonishing wealth of flowers. With the pleasures you forged pains. You took on the role of the august Being who governs. Space was then filled with a spirit of the cavern. You said to the Eternal:—There are two of us now!—You soiled Infinity by merely spying on it. Across the Ocean you blew shipwreck. Captive, you pierced the earth with your fury. The melancholy underside of life belonged to your vengeance, and was tainted by your breath. You gnawed on tombs, you gnawed on roots. You mixed perfumes with dead weeds; you placed everywhere the monster beside the law. A night emanation issued from you, and you dishonored the noble universe. God shone the good, you shone crime. You created in the nether regions, with your miasmas, demons. You took vile instincts and impure mud and created, from this clay, the traitorous, the cowardly, the malevolent; and you made gods and masters from creatures of the abyss and convict spirits. You impelled Nimrods to war, you pitted the Bloody Caiaphases against the sublime Christs; and often above, we, the angels, turned pale, hearing, during our bereavement, the priests and kings laughing, and seeing, growing ever larger, the enormous sword in the shape of a cross.

What purpose has it served? More suffering, that is all. Your flash of lightning eats away and burns your talons; your poisoning of the world began with yourself, O giant of senseless combat. Evil does not frighten God; God gets angry, and strikes. You believed that vengeance is sweet; it is bitter. Alas! Crime is punishment. The growth of evil increases your own agony; the evil you inflict adds to the evil you suffer. Your lava in the depth of the nights falls back upon you again as brimstone; and you yourself have at times been heard to confess it. Your torture of everything is going to revert to you. You make everything falter, everything tremble at its base, everything collapse, and it is you whom your effort crushes. All the Earth, at present, being beneath your yoke, see! you, yourself, are weighed down by more dread! See! You, yourself, are more deformed, and your brazen heart bleeds!

But, Satan, we must surely in the end pity you. You must see someone weeping, and so I come to you! I come to lament, but also to illumine, to enlighten, to at least remove the weight of the terrestrial chain, and cure the somber human wound in your side. My father, listen to me. For balm and for anodyne, to mix some joy with your dejection, you have till this hour, in your bitter Gehenna, tried only night, vengeance, and hatred. O wretched Titan, try, at last, daylight! Let the swan soar instead of you, O vulture! Let an angel taken from your wings waft upon the plagues an irresistible and tender breath. Let us raise Cain, who cowers atop Abel. Enough darkness and crime! Let us prevent Babel raising even higher its hideous coils. Oh! Let me reopen the sepulchral gates that, in the depths of Hell, you closed on the soul! Let me release man into Freedom. Let me reach out to the sinking universe. Let me knock down the mountain of shadows; let me pull down the vile tower of evil! Allow, through me, the world to return to the baptismal azure, so that Eden may reappear!

Alas! Do you feel my trembling heart that cherishes you? Do you hear me sobbing in your dungeon? Allow me to save the good, the pure, the innocent; let the soul take flight and suffering end. God made me Liberty; you, make me Deliverance! Oh! Do not forbid me to cast into the Heavens and Hells the factious cry

"You must see someone weeping, and so I come to you!"

"Let me release man into Freedom."

of love. Let me lavish on the terrestrial sphere the vast air, blue sky, boundless hope, and cause to emerge from the brow of Man an immeasurable beam of light. Let me save everything, I, your blessèd side! Consent!

Oh! I who emanate from you, allow me to go amongst the living, to complete this battle between their ignorance, alas! and their reason, to place a sacred crimson at the horizon, so that the hideous past may vanish into the darkness, so that the earth may tremble and the prison collapse, so that the eruption may take place, and so that finally Man may see, beyond the pain, hunger, war, kings, gods, insanity, the volcano of joy casting up its copious lava!

VIII

While this lovely virgin was speaking, like the breast giving milk drop by drop to the newborn child who sleeps with opened mouth, Satan, still floating like a leaf of grass in emerald water, stirred in the abyss, and seemed at times to tremble desperately in his sleep. Thus, as dawn breaks, then fades in a fog, so the devil got brighter, then turned pale, his face like a battlefield of gloom. The struggle between good and evil was revealed on it, an ebb and flow of two *stygian* armies. His sinister, closed lips twitched; his fists beat one against the other, becoming dark and monstrous. His eyes did not open, but beneath his heavy lids could be seen the glow of this strange soul, just as the thunderbolt turns the sky magenta behind a cloud. The angel watched him, her hands clasped. Finally a light that a seraph might have cast, radiated from this great, feverish brow. Like two rocks cleaving asunder, his lips parted, a thunderous breath lifted his dreadful flank, and the angel heard this word:—Go!

Denouement

Satan beneath his vault:—I draw myself up, marked by this appalling feature: (The last stage of the horror!)—Love hates me.

A Voice across the Infinite:—No, I do not hate you. We are related through an angel; what she did affects you. Man, enchained by you, by her is freed. O Satan, you need only say:—I shall live!—Come, the destroyed prison abolishes Hell! Come, the angel Liberty is both your daughter and mine. This sublime fatherhood unites us. The archangel again lives, and the devil is no more; I efface sinister night, and nothing of it remains. Satan is dead; be reborn, O celestial Lucifer! Come, arise out of the darkness with the dawn upon your brow!

BIBLIOGRAPHY

Austin, Lloyd James. *Poetic Principles and Practices: occasional papers on Baudelaire, Mallarmé, and Valéry*, chapter 8, "Mallarmé and the visual arts" (1972), Cambridge, New York: Cambridge University Press, 1987.

Blackmore, E. H. and A. M. unpublished MS of *Dieu* translation.

Druick, Douglas W. et al. *Odilon Redon: prince of dreams, 1840-1916*, [Chicago]: Art Institute of Chicago; [Amsterdam]: Van Gogh Museum; [London]: Royal Academy of Arts; [New York]: H.N. Abrams, Inc., 1994.

Frey, John Andrew. *A Victor Hugo Encyclopedia*. Westport, Connecticut: Greenwood Press, 1999.

Gamboni, Dario. *The Brush and the Pen: Odilon Redon and Literature*. Chicago: University of Chicago Press, 2011.

Gruber, Lucretia S. "Alfred de Vigny's 'Eloa': A Modern Myth." Modern Language Studies, vol. 6, no.1, Spring (1976): 74-82.

Hugo, Victor. *Dramas / Victor Hugo*; volume I, *Hernani*. Translated by I. G. Burnham. Philadelphia: George Barrie, 1896.

——.*Dramas / Victor Hugo*; volume IX, *Oliver Cromwell*. Translated by I.G. Burnham. Philadelphia: George Barrie, 1896.

——. *God* and *The End of Satan / Dieu et La Fin de Satan*: selections in a bilingual edition. Translated by R.G. Skinner. Chicago: Swan Isle Press, 2014.

——. *Novels / Victor Hugo*; volume III, *The Toilers of the Sea*. Translated by Mary W. Artois. Philadelphia: George Barrie, 1892.

——. *Œuvres complète de Victor Hugo, Poésie XI, La Fin de Satan. Dieu.* Paris: Imprimerie nationale, 1911.

——. *Œuvres de Victor Hugo,* volume XI: *Marion de Lorme. Hernani.* Brussels: Louis Hauman et Comp., 1832 .

——. *Poésie,* 3 volumes. Edited by Bernard Leuilliot. Paris: Éditions du Seuil, 1972.

——. *Victor Hugo: Selected Poetry.* Translated by Steven Monte. New York: Routledge, 2002.

——. *Victor Hugo, The Letters of Victor Hugo: From Exile, and After the Fall of the Empire.* Edited by Paul Meurice. Boston: Houghton Mifflin & Co., 1898.

Journet, René and Guy Robert. *Contribution aux études sur Victor Hugo: Le texte de "La Fin de Satan."* Paris: Belles Lettres, 1979.

Kramer, Hilton. "Art View: Symbolism—in search of a style." New York Times (Arts), January 4, 1981.

Redon, Odilon. *I am the First Consciousness of Chaos: the black album.* Edited by Candice Black. Washington D.C.: Solar Books, 2010.

Rodari, Florian. *Shadows of a Hand: the drawings of Victor Hugo.* Translated by Judith Hayward and Mark Hutchinson. London: The Drawing Center New York in association with Merrell Holberton Publishers, 1998.

Simon, Gustave. "Paul Meurice—souvenirs intimes" in *La Revue de Paris.* Treizième Année. Tome Troisième. Mai–Juin. Paris: Bureaux de la Revue de Paris, 1906.

Swinburne, Algernon Charles. *Studies in prose and poetry.* London: Chatto & Windus, 1894.

Swan Isle Press is a not-for-profit publisher
of poetry, fiction, and nonfiction.

For information on books of related interest or
for a catalog of new publications contact:
www.swanislepress.com

Satan and His Daughter, The Angel Liberty
Designed by Marianne Jankowski
Typeset in Adobe Jensen Pro
Printed on 55# Glatfelter Natural